Trees *of the* West

Trees *of the* West

AN ARTIST'S GUIDE MOLLY HASHIMOTO

SKIPSTONE

Published by Skipstone, an imprint of Mountaineers Books—an independent, nonprofit publisher. Skipstone and its colophon are registered trademarks of The Mountaineers organization.
Printed in China

25 24 23 22   1 2 3 4 5

Copyeditor: Laura Lancaster
Design: Kate Basart/Union Pageworks
Cover illustration: *Aspens at Yellowstone National Park*
Frontispiece: *Frijoles Creek, Bandelier Monument, New Mexico*
Page 192: *Fox and lodgepole pines, Yellowstone National Park*
Samuel Palmer's *Oak Trees, Lullingstone Park* on page 15 included with permission of National Gallery of Canada.

Library of Congress Control Number: 2022933078

Printed on FSC®-certified materials

ISBN (hardcover): 978-1-68051-338-7

Skipstone books may be purchased for corporate, educational, or other promotional sales, and our authors are available for a wide range of events. For information on special discounts or booking an author, contact our customer service at 800.553.4453 or mbooks@mountaineersbooks.org.

Skipstone
1001 SW Klickitat Way
Suite 201
Seattle, Washington 98134
206.223.6303
www.skipstonebooks.org
www.mountaineersbooks.org

LIVE LIFE. MAKE RIPPLES.

To Tom, Rose, *and* Paul *and in memory of* David

Contents

Northern Coastal & Cascade Forests

California Redwood Forests

Woodlands

California Coastal Forests, Chaparral & Scrub

Introduction: First Trees

Nature is painting for us, day after day, pictures of infinite beauty if only we have the eyes to see them.

—**John Ruskin**

My first trees were the conifers of the Rockies near Denver, and their scent will always transport me to my earliest years. Once I remember waiting for the school bus when I was about six years old, in what seemed a world without time, completely focused on watching a squirrel scurry up a tree. I probably sat there for an hour, searching the leafy branches for the busy little creature, before I realized that I had missed the bus. I had a daydreaming propensity even then, which the world of nature and the outdoors fostered.

Later, when I was eleven and living with my family on the Fort Bragg army base in North Carolina, we had a maple tree in the backyard, not too tall, nor large, that invited climbing. I could get up to a safe perch about twelve feet off the ground, and I used to like to sit up there, hidden by leaves, watching the goings-on of my family and other neighbors. We had a big family, so three of us younger girls slept in army-issued triple bunk beds in one room. There was never any privacy—not that children really expect that—and there was a lot of drama in the house, arguing, unhappiness, maybe more than the average family. The tree felt like a friend, a helper, and it offered me a kind of solitude, a way to get perspective, a way to be soothed by a non-human living being. Of course I didn't really think all those thoughts at the time, only that it was fun to get up in the tree and be far away. Eventually we moved to Minnesota, where two large oak trees embraced our second-floor bedroom. At night, when the noise from the trucks on Highway 7 kept me awake, I loved the sound of the oak leaves in the wind, brushing up against the house with their stiff leaf hands.

When I look back, I understand the profound effect that those trees had on me, how they comforted me in my city life, without my being conscious of their very separate lives. Now it is clear that for me they are the interface between urban and wilderness, and that they are necessary for my well-being. They invite me to look further, to investigate their wildness, even within a city or suburb, and beckon me to the wild places beyond cities. I both sketch them on location and commit them to my memory through photographs and close attention, and then create studio paintings of them once I am at home. I consider these trees portals to health, healing, the world of the imagination, and the wild.

SUGAR PINE

The Biogeography of Trees

Continental drift and past climate conditions have played a part in determining where flora and fauna are distributed throughout the world—their biogeography. Researchers called biohistorians look into the past history of the planet in order to understand the current distribution of species. Working with scientists, including botanists and biologists studying present-day distribution, they have designated distinct biogeographic regions, as well as smaller ecoregions and biomes within biogeographic regions.

The chapters in this book look at trees in the following biogeographic regions of the West: northern coastal and Cascade forests; California redwood forests; woodlands (subdivided into northern, California, and Southwest woodlands); California coastal forests, chaparral, and scrub; Rocky Mountain forests; giant sequoia groves; subalpine forests (subdivided into northern and southern regions); and deserts (including the Great Basin, Mojave, Sonoran, and Chihuahuan).

Plant communities living in similar environments around the world can contain the same types or even species of trees. That's because particular climatic and geologic conditions will only support species that adapt specific strategies for survival. A good example is the larch family. Larches are common in the high mountains of western North America, but they are also found in the Alps and in the Himalaya. These high-altitude environments have cold winters and extreme solar radiation, which are usually not tolerated by lowland species. The larch is one of the few deciduous conifers, meaning it loses its needles in the winter. This is a useful adaptation, as the branches would break under heavy snow if the needles were not shed.

An ecotone is an interesting biogeographic designation, particularly as it relates to trees. It is the area between two plant communities, a kind of boundary zone where species from two biomes mix. At times, a species in one biome can overtake the species of the other biome, changing the very conditions of that other biome. In the West, it is common for subalpine firs to invade alpine meadows; this is currently taking place at Paradise in Mount Rainier National Park due to warming climate conditions. Meadows there are considered by some to be the finest wildflower garden in the world. There, trees are establishing colonies in the meadow zone, casting deep shadows on sun-loving plants. The consequence is fewer of the beloved wildflowers that make Paradise such a destination, as well as fewer plants for insects to pollinate.

Although this book's chapters organize trees of the West by biogeographical region, many of the tree species described here live in several of these regions. A good example is the Douglas-fir, an extremely adaptable tree that grows from Canada to Mexico and from the Pacific coast to the Rockies. In some cases I chose to write about a tree in only one biogeographical region, even though it is widespread throughout the West.

Another key factor influencing where a particular tree species can be found in the West, as well as what form it takes, is the changing location of timberline. Timberline (the altitude above which no trees can grow) varies geographically on a north-south axis as well as an east-west axis,

Biogeographical Tree Regions of the West

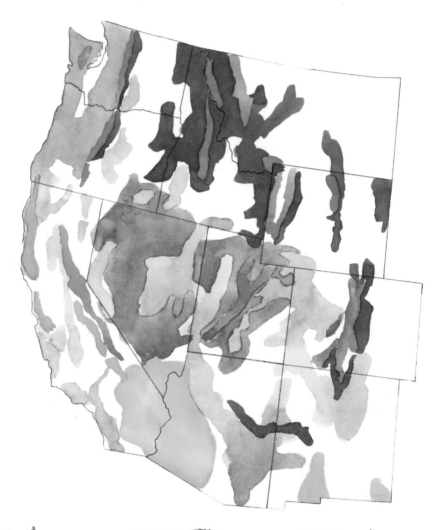

NORTHERN COASTAL & CASCADES FORESTS

CALIFORNIA COASTAL FORESTS

SUBALPINE FORESTS

REDWOOD FORESTS

ROCKY MOUNTAIN FORESTS

GREAT BASIN DESERT

WOODLANDS

GIANT SEQUOIA GROVES

SOUTHWEST DESERTS

depending on the region. In the North Cascades, timberline is at 5,500 feet, while it's 7,500 feet in the central Oregon Cascades, 10,000 feet in the northern Sierra Nevada, and 11,000 feet in Southern California. The timberline of the Rockies varies as well, with Glacier National Park at 6,900 feet on the west slope, the Tetons at 10,000 feet, the Colorado Rockies at 11,000 to 12,000 feet, and New Mexico at 12,000 feet. One example of how timberline affects trees is in the range of the whitebark pine in California. In the southern Sierra, it grows up to sixty feet tall between 9,000 and 11,000 feet, but between 11,000 and 12,000 feet it only grows as a stunted tree (krummholz). Farther north in California in the Klamath Ranges and on Mount Shasta the whitebark pine grows at 8,000 to 9,500 feet, again becoming a krummholz specimen when it reaches the limits of tree line in more severe conditions.

Alexander von Humboldt and the *Naturgemälde*

The German scientist Alexander von Humboldt was a brilliant geographer, explorer, and naturalist whose work established the foundation for biogeography and a more complex way of viewing the natural world. He traveled to South America in 1799 in order to study the plant life and geology. The crowning event of that trip was his June 1802 ascent of Mount Chimborazo, a 20,564-foot Andean volcano. It is in fact the highest point on Earth, given that it is only one degree south of the equator, where the earth bulges. While climbing the mountain, Humboldt saw many species

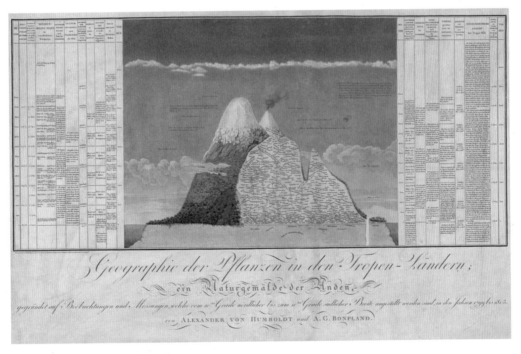

NATURGEMÄLDE, ALEXANDER VON HUMBOLDT

that had counterparts in other alpine regions that he had visited, like the Swiss Alps. This led him to develop the idea of ecosystems. Instead of isolating plants in taxonomic categories, he viewed them in the context of their elevation, climate, and soil type. Humboldt wasn't as interested in uncovering new facts as he was in creating a fluid and connected system where all things were related. "Nature is a living whole," he said, not a "dead aggregate." While still in the Andean foothills, he created a sketch of the *Naturgemälde* ("painting of nature") and then in 1808 published it as a full-color three-foot-by-two-foot drawing. He felt this art explained almost everything that he had discovered. It is still an amazing creation more than two hundred years later, a combination of science, language, and art that showed all the plants on this enormous mountain, revealing how each one had its own ideal growing location, depending on elevation. I find his combination of art and science inspiring—not only did he see connections between plants and animals and place, but as a true polymath, a nineteenth-century Leonardo, he was able to bring his ideas to life through art.

When I moved to Seattle in my early twenties, I spent most of my free time in the mountains. It was there that I had my own experience of the *Naturgemälde* as I became aware of the different species growing in the mountains. As I ascended it was utterly obvious that certain tree species were confined to certain elevations, and then I noticed that some of the more widespread species changed shape and sometimes size at higher and higher elevations.

In my garden in Seattle I have grown many native trees and plants, including two favorites. The bristlecone pine, which seems very happy in a pot on the deck, looks so much like a bonsai specimen—people admire it, yet I had very little to do with its appearance. It grows as it would in the harshest conditions in the wild: rather stubby, with short needles and slightly bent branches (see the pen and watercolor sketch in Subalpine Forests chapter). The other tree is the lodgepole pine Chief Joseph, which was discovered in the Wallowa Mountains in eastern Oregon and named for Chief Joseph in honor of the Nez Perce homeland in that area.

Tree Journeys and Fortresses

Some years back, I wrote in my journal:

> *Walking near Indian Creek and Swan Lake at Yellowstone, I looked west towards Quadrant and Antler Peaks, and saw only the tiniest patches of snow up high. I remembered in earlier years on this exact date seeing much more snow. I tried not to feel the now-familiar realization that it was another sign of our changing world, but rather chose to see it as evidence of a world that would become a different place after my short life span—short when compared to the deep time of the planet. Different plants would grow, trees might move up or down gullies depending on whether they could survive in that new and warmer world. One species might die out altogether, the way Alaska cedars did in all but the coolest north-facing ravines in central Oregon, where they now exist only as relict populations—and another more adaptable tree, like the Douglas-fir, which at present ranges from British Columbia to southern Mexico, might thrive more fully there. We don't often think of trees moving—they seem such stable inhabitants of the world. But in geological time, trees race east and west across mountain ranges, and north and south along the coasts.*

The very first trees appeared on Earth 400 million years ago. As trees evolved, the gymnosperms, including the conifers, flourished. During the Jurassic Period, around 140 million years ago, the landscape was dominated by huge trees, like the sequoia, and during that period there may have been as many as 20,000 species of conifer (there are now only 630). By around 100 million years ago, the conifers were beginning to be displaced by angiosperms, or broadleaved trees,

because of this new genus's competitive advantage. According to Aljos Farjon, author of *A Natural History of Conifers*, "per unit the leaves and wood vessels of angiosperms are more efficient in their respective tasks than the needles and tracheids of conifers. Wood vessels transport water more efficiently and the greater surface and more elaborate venation of angiosperm leaves allow higher rates of assimilation." Because the conifers, or gymnosperms, grow more slowly, the broadleaved trees achieve greater height faster, blocking sunlight; as they grow larger they claim a greater share of water and nutrients.

But the conifers did become very adept at growing where the broadleaved trees, which require richer soils, less extreme temperatures, and more consistent moisture, could not survive. It isn't just animals that compete and experience predation. Plants and trees do as well, and to survive, they must develop strategies or seek habitats and conditions that put them at an advantage, or protect from competition and predation. Farjon calls the locales with poor conditions "fortresses." For the gymnosperms, these conditions include high altitude, aridity, poor soils, extreme radiation, and wind. Conifers have important advantages over the leafiest trees. One is that they accumulate needles over several generations so that their foliage eventually has more total surface area for absorbing sunlight and water; meanwhile, in winter, the broadleaved trees are bare of leaves and dormant. Another advantage is the mycorrhizal networks found in the poor soils where conifers live, allowing the trees to take up nutrients. In the fertile soils where the broadleaved trees thrive, these rich networks of fungi are much reduced.

As the earth has undergone climate changes, conifers have ventured in and out of their fortresses—seeking places where they could thrive—journeys that paleobotanists now study. The fortresses to which the conifers have retreated today are found throughout the world, most notably in the Northern Hemisphere in boreal and montane forests, but these fortresses exist in many other parts of the world as well.

Artists and Trees

If you can paint one leaf, you can paint the world.   —**John Ruskin,** from *Modern Painters*

By the time of the Tang dynasty in China, around 600 CE, nature subjects with symbolic meanings in paintings and other art forms had become very popular. Pine trees, with beautifully rendered twisted trunks and boughs, could be emblematic of survival in challenging political circumstances or could remind viewers of the good fortune of scholars and poets who lived to old age. Inspired by Chinese art, Hasegawa Tohaku painted pines in Japan during the late sixteenth century, representing them in a very formalized style, as minimalist, restrained, and meditative as Zen Buddhism.

Although trees had been represented in pre-Christian and Christian art in Europe, where they were associated with life and the afterlife, they did not merit attention on their own as subjects until the eighteenth century. British artist Paul Sandby painted the first tree portrait in 1794: *Ancient Beech Tree*, a striking watercolor in the collection of the Victoria and Albert Museum. What I consider the apotheosis of tree portraiture was painted by another British artist, Samuel Palmer, in 1828: *Oak Trees, Lullingstone Park*. Palmer struggled with this painting, which he created on commission for another artist, John Linnell, who helped to support his work and encouraged nature study. Palmer wrote to Linnell of his attempt to avoid the distractions of "the moss, and rifts, and barky furrows" and to catch the "grasp and grapple of the roots, the muscular belly and shoulders, the twisted sinews." One hears a bit of anthropomorphizing here, as well as an echo of William Blake, who saw animate forms in nature.

Palmer belonged to a loose group of artists who called themselves the Ancients, so called because they believed that the classical world was superior to modern civilization, with its turn toward industrialization. Some of their art may have been described as leaning toward primitivism. They looked up to Blake as a kind of father figure, although they rejected his more radical ideas, since their return to ancient order predisposed them to rather conservative politics. Blake was a true visionary and saw nature as emblematic of a higher spiritual reality. Although Palmer did not experience visions, he did attempt to fashion art that was innovative and powerful, inspired by the poetry of another of his heroes, John Milton. A short-lived movement, the Ancients were forerunners of the Pre-Raphaelites,

OAK TREES, LULLINGTONE PARK, SAMUEL PALMER (NATIONAL GALLERY OF CANADA, OTTAWA)

Nalini Nadkarni, Forest Ecologist

Nalini Nadkarni is a forest ecologist and biology professor at the University of Utah with a special interest in the arts. She's been studying forests, trees, and their connections to human beings for most of her career. After receiving a bachelor of science degree from Brown University and a PhD from the College of Forest Resources at the University of Washington, she conducted research on tropical and temperate rainforests, exploring the little-known world of the canopy and the creatures that inhabit it. She has also been concerned with the effects of logging on forest health and biodiversity, as well as its effects on the human communities that rely on it. She is a strong supporter of the arts and has striven throughout her career to connect artists of all kinds with scientists in order to foster awareness and conservation efforts. In her wonderful book *Between Earth and Sky: Our Intimate Connections to Trees*, she writes of trees as both a scientist and a lover of the arts. She explains the services trees provide, the health they engender, the symbols that have formed around them in human culture, and their spiritual significance, enriching the text on almost every page with poetry.

FOREST AT ROCKPORT STATE PARK, WASHINGTON

who would rekindle interest in Blake. Celebrated British watercolorists John Constable, J. M. W. Turner, and John Sell Cotman also honored trees in their iconic landscape paintings.

There are a number of North American artists who made trees the primary focus of powerful paintings, such as Thomas Moran, of the Hudson River School, whose Yellowstone paintings helped establish our first national park in 1872. Canadian Emily Carr painted groundbreaking portraits of western redcedars and other native Pacific Northwest species beginning around 1910. As the twentieth century unfolded, Gustave Baumann of Santa Fe celebrated aspens and pines in his color woodcuts, and Californian William S. Rice created striking block print portraits of a number of unique pines, junipers, and sequoias in the Sierra. Also working at this time were two notable artists based in Bellingham, Washington. Elizabeth Colborne made mountains, Douglas-firs, and hemlocks the subjects of her beautiful block prints, following in the Japanese tradition. Helen Loggie, a timber heiress, made etchings and incredibly precise and elegant pencil drawings of Washington native trees, including cedars and junipers.

One of my favorite recent representations of trees, imagined by artist John Grade, hangs in the Brotman Forum of the Seattle Art Museum. *Middle Fork* is a magnificent life-sized sculpture of a 140-year-old western hemlock from the Cascade Range. To create this work, Grade and volunteers made a full-sized plaster cast of the living tree and then recreated it from thousands of pieces of reclaimed old growth cedar.

TOWNSEND'S CHIPMUNK

Voices of the Forest

Trees are the most civil society. —**Robert Louis Stevenson,** from *An Inland Voyage*

In his essay "The Forest Is the Polis," philosopher Justin E. H. Smith writes that a "traditional Amazonian society, which seems extremely simple to the unknowing outsider, comes to appear far more complex than a modern nation-state once we realize that it includes not only human beings as its members, but also parrots and monkeys and boars and insects and all the countless varieties of tree and brush that make up the rainforest's ground and canopy. In such a society, all of these beings are 'persons,' not human persons, but nonetheless actors within a unified sociocosmic whole. The forest 'is' the polis."

The term *polis* originally referred to the city-state in ancient Greece, especially its ideal form as it was elaborated in philosophy. More broadly, it refers to a body of citizens with a shared sense of community. Various cultures have expanded their idea of the polis to include nonhumans as "citizens." In New

Trees for All

Spending time with trees and walking in forests, what the Japanese call "forest bathing," is extremely important for human health. Studies have proven that taking walks in the forest lowers blood pressure, heart rate, and stress hormones. At the same time, it decreases anxiety, depression, and fatigue. Visiting forests may also decrease inflammation, a proven cause of disease. Unfortunately, it is becoming the norm *not* to go outside. Studies have shown the average adult spends eleven and a half hours a day consuming media.

Dr. Nooshin Razani, a pediatrician and researcher at UCSF Benioff Children's Hospital in Oakland, California, runs a monthly program that helps urban children get a dose of nature. In a randomized trial of seventy-eight families conducted in 2018, Dr. Razani found that every park visit, which she calls "park prescriptions," decreased families' stress and increased children's resilience.

One of the obstacles to experiencing nature is the lack of tree canopy in many cities. Canopy describes the trees throughout a city, including backyards, streets, and parks. Most people encounter nature in their own neighborhoods; many families can't afford camping and hiking trips out of the city. In neighborhoods with a high rate of poverty, there is 25 percent less tree canopy than in neighborhoods with higher incomes. In fact, some studies of extreme disparities have shown that in some wealthy areas, there are 65 percent more trees compared to communities where nine out of ten people live below the poverty line. Neighborhoods lacking trees also lose the many benefits trees provide. A University of Illinois Urbana-Champaign study of ninety-eight Chicago public housing buildings with residents in similar socioeconomic situations found that when there is more vegetation near a building, there are 52 percent fewer crimes overall and 56 percent fewer violent crimes. (This according to a July 4, 2021, article "Since When Have Trees Existed Only for Rich Americans," in the *New York Times*.) Trees also keep temperatures up to ten degrees cooler, which is significant, since mortality increases with hotter temperatures.

The disparity in tree canopy is the result of the historic redlining of communities where poor people lived—mortgages were harder to obtain, as well as health care, food services, and infrastructure investment. It also resulted in a failure to create parks and plant boulevard trees. Redlining took place in many cities across the country; Black, Catholic, Jewish, Latino, and immigrant communities suffered as a result, and there has not been any redress for the current residents of those neighborhoods. The Urban and Community Forestry Program, supported by House Bill 1216, passed on April 12, 2021. Among other goals, it seeks to increase tree canopy cover, density, and spacing. The Tree Equity Score estimated that 522 million more trees will need to be planted in order to achieve equity in all neighborhoods.

What can we do? Joining a local tree-planting organization such as One Tree Planted, Trees for the Future, or the International Tree Foundation is a good way to begin to right this wrong, as well as voting for elected officials who support better infrastructure for all.

HERITAGE TREE: SCARLET OAK IN SEATTLE

Zealand, rivers and lands have recently been granted legal personhood in accordance with Maori traditional beliefs. One particular area, Te Urewera, is a notable example, where even the mist is a person.

Those of us who live in the West can learn to listen to what Smith calls the "submerged voices" of our communities of trees, whether they are in our parks and backyards or in our wild places. We can understand and appreciate that all of nature is speaking to us. With *Trees of the West*, I aim to honor all of the West's forests and trees—young and old, common and rare, wherever their location, and whether cherished as a "champion tree" (those with a long history or stupendous size) or as a backyard friend. In addition to the featured species in each chapter, I also list many other trees found in the region, as well as some common understory plants, birds, mammals, and other creatures.

The Art of Trees: Methods and Materials

All of us can learn to listen to the "voices" of trees by observing the natural world, by paying attention, listening, touching, and inhaling the scents. Drawings, prints, paintings, and etchings further give voice to these communities of living beings. And if we create these artworks ourselves, we have further tools beyond our senses. With photographs, sketches, paintings, and written works like essays and poetry, we can use our art to deepen our understanding. And for me, it is a way of paying homage to the beauty of trees and forests, whether I am outdoors painting *en plein air* (French for "in the open air"), or back at home in my studio.

SKETCHING

When sketching with a pencil, I like to use a smooth paper or one with not too much "tooth," or texture. Paper labeled "cold press" is bumpy; "hot press" is smooth. It's best if the pencil doesn't encounter too many bumps in the road, which can make for a broken line. I want to choose when to break the line, not have the paper do that! If you're planning to add watercolor later, select a hot press watercolor paper or a sketchbook with a somewhat heavier smooth paper as a lighter weight paper will buckle once water is applied.

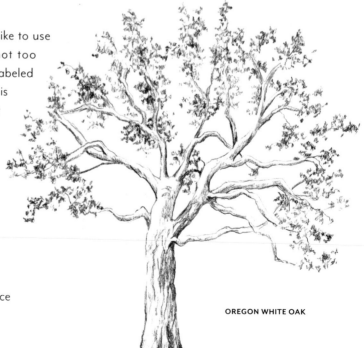

OREGON WHITE OAK

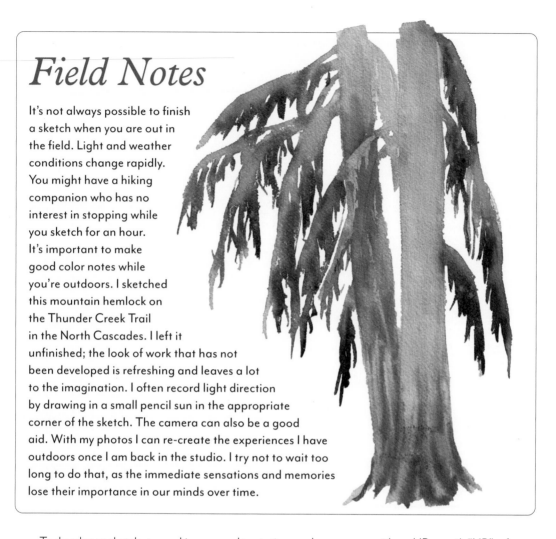

Field Notes

It's not always possible to finish a sketch when you are out in the field. Light and weather conditions change rapidly. You might have a hiking companion who has no interest in stopping while you sketch for an hour. It's important to make good color notes while you're outdoors. I sketched this mountain hemlock on the Thunder Creek Trail in the North Cascades. I left it unfinished; the look of work that has not been developed is refreshing and leaves a lot to the imagination. I often record light direction by drawing in a small pencil sun in the appropriate corner of the sketch. The camera can also be a good aid. With my photos I can re-create the experiences I have outdoors once I am back in the studio. I try not to wait too long to do that, as the immediate sensations and memories lose their importance in our minds over time.

To do a loose sketch, try making several tentative marks on paper with an HB pencil. "HB" refers to the degree of darkness—H pencils are harder, B are softer, so HB is in the middle range. (The full spectrum goes from 7H to 8B. The higher the number of H, the lighter the value; conversely, the higher the number of B, the darker the value.) Don't feel as if you're committing to the line, just put it down quickly, making a series of marks or strokes that feel loosely connected. Once you've completed the perimeter of the tree shape, stand back and see if your proportions look right. It often takes standing back to see that perhaps the trunk is too large and thick for the crown shape of the tree—a common beginner issue. Feel free to erase and reposition lines if necessary. Then, once you're satisfied, use a slightly darker pencil, like a 2B or even darker, and go over the lines. Shade in the darker areas of the trunk and leaves or needles with a 5B pencil. The whole idea with a sketch is that it's free and loose and not totally finished. That unfinished quality is what makes it so lively.

WATERCOLOR

Watercolor is the quickest painting medium to execute: you can make a quick pencil sketch, wet a sheet of watercolor paper, mix up all the colors you see in a landscape, and fill in the sketch in five or ten minutes. Edges won't be defined because you are using a wet-into-wet method, but because you can be outdoors while you do this, the colors will be more accurate. This is not possible in any other medium. Watercolor can express mist, rain, and fog, as well as the multiple greens of a forest. European artists have been using watercolor for studies since Albrecht Durer's landscapes and plant and animal paintings in the fifteenth century. It's a way to try out ideas, sample colors. And more than that, watercolor is an accessible medium, inexpensive, easy to try out, easy to set up—I think of it as a very democratic medium. It doesn't have to be done in a studio—outdoors or a kitchen table work fine, and major technical training is not a prerequisite.

One of my favorite things about watercolor is that it is nontoxic. Also, even though it's now becoming more common to clean up oil paints with oil—a practice of Renaissance painters—oil paints are usually cleaned up with solvents. (In the eighteenth century, painters quickly switched to these new inventions, a by-product of the Industrial Revolution, since they made cleaning so easy, but solvents are very hard on the environment and painters alike). Watercolor, on the other hand, rinses clean in water and cleans up in minutes.

MADRONA ON LOPEZ ISLAND, WASHINGTON

I paint in my watercolor sketchbooks in many different ways. I cut Arches paper into a 10" x 13" size and then make sketchbooks, which allow for every type of work. The hard cover and spiral binding mean that it can be opened out in the field with no support, in order to do *plein air* drawing and painting on one page, or spread out to two pages for a large panoramic landscape. Arches 140 lb. watercolor paper is 100 percent rag, and is double-sized, so you have more working time, and you can wipe out mistakes. I also appreciate the fact that by primarily using this size and type of sketchbook, there is a semblance of structure in my life and in my studio. I label them so I know where to find sketches, and they sit on a shelf together in chronological order, giving me a sense of accomplishment (however illusory!). Once you begin keeping sketchbooks or journals, you realize the importance of recording experiences and ideas—it is a very personal endeavor, but it is one that makes you a more thoughtful participant in the landscapes you venture to see.

Here's what I bring when I have time to paint for half an hour or more: HB pencil, plastic eraser, sketchbook, ¾" flat sable watercolor brush, ½" flat synthetic brush, #4 and #6 round sable water-color brushes, and a lightweight plastic palette loaded with the paints I list in "Mixing Colors" on page 24. (It's safest to squeeze them into the plastic palette a few days before heading out, so they get a chance to dry—otherwise they can leak out while still runny.) I put them on the uphill side of the slanted palette wells, and then when I use them, add water and let the wash of color float down to the bottom of the well. The paints start with yellow and go counterclockwise around the palette: hansa yellow light, hansa yellow medium, hansa yellow deep, yellow ochre, quinacridone gold, quinacridone burnt orange, pyrrol scarlet, perylene red, permanent alizarin crimson, quinacridone magenta, carbazole violet, phthalo green, perylene green, phthalo blue green shade, phthalo blue red shade, French ultramarine blue, cobalt blue, indanthrone blue. I have pictured a few tubes that I bring with me for longer outings—hansa yellow medium and deep and quinacridone burnt orange are colors I go through a lot of.

Mixing Colors

You can do a multitude of things with watercolor—quick sketches, finished paintings, add it to pen and acrylic, and tint prints and etchings with it. Just knowing a few basics about color mixing will equip you with enough knowledge to use it for your sketches and prints. In the color wheel you see two of each primary color:

YELLOW: hansa yellow deep and hansa yellow medium.

BLUE: phthalo blue green shade and phthalo blue red shade.

RED: permanent alizarin crimson and pyrrol scarlet.

With these you can mix secondary colors. For a warm orange, mix hansa yellow deep and pyrrol scarlet. For a violet, mix permanent alizarin crimson and phthalo blue red shade. For green, mix hansa yellow medium and phthalo blue green shade.

Notice on the color wheel just how many possibilities there are within each third of the pie. Some lean more toward one color. You will also see this on the green mixture chart. I often add a bit of quinacridone burnt orange to my green mixtures. Most greens in nature are not quite as vivid as pure secondary hues and need to be neutralized just a little bit. Another way to achieve neutrals is to cross the line on the color wheel—any time you mix by using a color across the line, you will get something a bit more neutral. So I use hansa yellow medium and phthalo blue

red shade (rather than phthalo blue green shade, which would get me a much brighter green). Another way to get a neutral green is to add a very small amount of permanent alizarin crimson to your mixture of hansa yellow medium and phthalo blue. Broadleaved trees tend to have foliage that is much brighter in hue than conifers, which can lean more toward blue, and are often darker and more saturated.

Colors that are adjacent to each other on the color wheel are called harmonious or analogous colors. Mixing them gives you clean, bright mixtures. Colors opposite one another are called complementary colors, and mixing them gives you some very interesting neutral hues—try it out, and you'll discover intriguing grays, browns, and muddy greens. There are no rights and wrongs in color

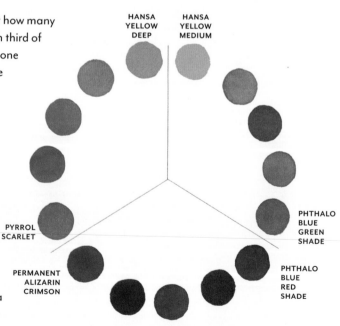

HANSA YELLOW DEEP
HANSA YELLOW MEDIUM
PHTHALO BLUE GREEN SHADE
PHTHALO BLUE RED SHADE
PYRROL SCARLET
PERMANENT ALIZARIN CRIMSON

HANSA YELLOW
MEDIUM

PHTHALO BLUE
RED SHADE

QUINACRIDONE
BURNT ORANGE

COTTONWOOD AND COLONIAL PEAK, FALL COLOR

mixing. Try everything, and make notes about which colors you used; those notes will come in handy for future painting sessions!

Finally, here are a few ideas for tube paints to try out for fall color:

YELLOW: hansa yellow medium, hansa yellow deep (or try Winsor yellows), new gamboge, Indian yellow.

ORANGE: pyrrol orange, perinone orange.

SCARLET: pyrrol scarlet, scarlet lake.

RED: perylene red, permanent alizarin crimson.

MAROON: perylene maroon, quinacridone magenta mixed with quinacridone burnt orange.

VIOLET: carbazole violet, quinacridone magenta, quinacridone purple.

BROWN: quinacridone burnt orange, burnt sienna, burnt umber.

The first two columns on the chart above show a sampling of the many shades of green you can create by mixing phthalo blue red shade and hansa yellow medium. The third column illustrates what can be achieved by adding a little quinacridone burnt orange to the mixtures of the other two colors.

I've included many examples in the book of casual sketches that are hand-colored with watercolor in a fresh, unlabored way. But I have seen and experienced many other trees that demanded greater care and attention, and for those I create studio paintings, using sketches and photos as my references.

PRINTMAKING

When paper was introduced to Europe in the eleventh century, woodcut printing became an economical way to reproduce multiple pictures for the market, making images and texts affordable for a larger segment of the population. In this art form, images are drawn directly or transferred onto a wood block. The wood surrounding the outline (imagine a pen line) is then carved away, in reverse, which can be a little confusing, especially when words are part of the design. The outline of the figure or the letter remains raised, or in relief, so that a brayer or brush loaded with ink that is rolled or brushed across the block will leave a residue on the raised line. When paper is laid on the block, only the raised line prints. In the twenty-first century, images can be carved into linoleum (known as linocuts), wood, rubber, or any soft material—even a bar of soap! The resulting print is called a relief print. (The terms *block print* and *relief print* are interchangeable and can refer to any material.)

The earliest woodcut prints—images of saints and other religious figures—came from Germany and were sold as pilgrims' souvenirs at shrines and fairs; travelers collected mementos from their trips, very much as we do today. But early pilgrims also carried them as amulets on their journeys, to protect themselves from the plague or other misfortunes, and often kept them at home as well. Many of the earliest woodcut images have been found pasted into small travel chests. These simple figures were crudely carved, though full of strong line work, and contrasted notably with the high art achieved by later wood engravers such as Albrecht Durer.

After working as a watercolor artist for years, I tried carving rubber blocks (a soft material very similar to linoleum but much easier to carve) as an introduction to printmaking and fell in love with it after my very first carving. I found it was a way to create art with high values contrast, something not easily achieved in watercolor. With watercolor, edges are blurred, much is based on subtle gradations, and color can be somewhat weaker. With a block print, lines have clearly defined edges, and when black is used, the contrast between it and other colors is even greater. I also appreciate how tactile the three dimensions of the carving block and the carving tools are—it's as close to sculpting as I've yet come, and it's deeply satisfying.

While the process for creating block prints involves a number of steps, it is relatively simple.

ETCHING

Etching is also called *intaglio* printmaking; the word derives from the Italian verb *intagliare*, which means "to engrave" or "to cut." The lines you see in the final artwork are created by incising lines in metal plates. These incised lines will fill when ink is applied. The process is exactly the opposite of relief printmaking in which the lines themselves stand out in relief from the wood. Nineteenth-century artist James McNeill Whistler actually brought his plates outdoors and drew *en plein air*, quite an accomplishment with a studio technique like etching—few other artists had the nerve to try that! Venice was a favorite subject, and Whistler captured all the beauty and drama of its canals and architecture.

TECHNIQUE
Making a Block Print

Quick sketch with marker and watercolor or colored pencil: I often create a sketch very quickly using a waterproof bold marker and watercolor on Bristol paper, a heavyweight smooth paper strong enough to absorb a light wash without disintegrating. The pen is black and bold, so it makes heavy lines such as you'd see in a finished carved print, and the Bristol paper is inexpensive—this is, after all, just a sketch to try things out. But sometimes I've used a very lightweight paper that would not take kindly to a wet watercolor wash for my first sketch; such was the case here when I wanted to try out colors. I was already sure about the tree and landscape, so after I'd refined the drawing,

I used colored pencils to explore the colors. The pen line is black and bold and simulates what the relief print will look like before color is added.

Drawing for block print: The drawing refines the concept I explored in the quick marker and colored pencil sketch. Once I'm happy with the drawing, done in an HB pencil, I use a very dark pencil (a 5B) to redraw over the lighter pencil lines. Then I flip the drawing onto the carving block and rub it with a heavyweight kitchen spoon to transfer the image onto the block.

Carved block: Here you see the finished block with the areas that will be painted, or will remain white, carved away. The outline is now in relief, ready to print. The carved contours help to describe both the landscape contours and the tree foliage shapes and trunk texture.

Inking the block: In printing, I don't use relief inks, which I find don't come in the beautiful

QUICK SKETCH WITH MARKER

CARVED BLOCK

range of colors I like to choose from. Instead, I use high-quality oil-based etching ink (soft black, ivory black, or carbon black), which will resist—i.e., not bleed into—the watercolor I'll use later to tint the print; as the saying goes, oil and water don't mix! I like to thin the etching ink with a little bit of burnt plate oil. You want an ink consistency that is fairly gooey, not stiff, and if the ink is an etching ink (as opposed to a relief ink), depending on the color, as different colors have different degrees of viscosity, you may need to add more or less burnt plate oil to thin it out a bit. This reduces the "tack" of the ink. I use ½ tablespoon of burnt plate oil to 2 tablespoons of ink.

Using an ink knife, I spread the ink on a piece of plexiglass (I prefer plexi to glass because I don't have to worry about it

breaking) to about the width of the brayer. Then I roll the brayer back and forth on the plexi until I obtain a thin layer of ink sufficient to cover the brayer but not completely overload it. Next I roll the brayer onto the block, first horizontally and then vertically. Going in both directions ensures good coverage.

Printing: I place a good-quality hot press watercolor paper on the block and then rub vigorously with a heavyweight kitchen spoon. I gently lift up one corner of the print to see how well the image is transferring to the paper. If coverage is too light, I hold down the upper half of the print firmly, lift up the lower half, and reapply ink. I reverse this process for the upper half.

There's no need to clean the block between prints; you can leave the ink on and reapply with the brayer for each additional print.

UNTINTED PRINT

FINAL TINTED BLOCK PRINT

Editioning a print: Many printmakers do an entire edition, or set of prints, at once; 25 is considered a standard edition, but you can make anywhere from 5 to 500. Printmakers often label their prints below the actual artwork with the title, signature, and a set of two numbers—for example, 1/25. The first number refers to the number of the print in an edition, the second to the total number of prints in the edition. If you make all 25 prints at once, you number them up to 25/25. If you're not sure what additional artistic touches you will add to finish the print, you can label it AP, which stands for "artist's proof." Usually you make no more than 5 of those before making your final artistic decisions. If you think the edition is going to be quite variable because of factors outside of your control, such as maintaining a consistent hue, you can label the print EV, which stands for "edition variable," along with the number of prints.

Because my hand-tinted prints are so very handmade, I generally print only a few at a time. It can be wasteful to use twenty-five pieces of paper to make prints that may never sell, as you never know how the public will respond to the print; I print only as many as I need. Many artists do the same—there's no rule that says you have to print an entire edition at once. But I decide at printing time how many I'll eventually be making, and I do not increase that number—even if the print proves to be very popular. It would be unfair to the collectors who buy my prints to decide later that I'm going to make more prints from a block; generally, the smaller the edition, the more valuable the print. Also, near the end of the print edition, as in 24/25 or 25/25, it becomes obvious that all the other prints have been sold; thus, the remaining ones may be seen as worth more.

Unpainted print: Notice how the print is a mirror image of the carved block.

Tinting the block print: There are different ways to introduce color into a print. The block can be printed with oil-based black ink and then tinted by applying watercolor with a brush (see the "Watercolor" section above). Or the block can be printed with a colored ink. If only one color is chosen, then one block is sufficient, but if multiple areas with different colors are required, then it's necessary to carve multiple blocks, with each block dedicated to a specific color. (To get each block to line up, or "register," you create a registration template and lay the block on it before running it through the press; for more information, see *The Encyclopedia of Printmaking Techniques*, listed in "Further Reading.") When I tint with watercolor, I'm careful to accentuate the bright colors, since the strong blacks require intense color for balance. Often, leaving a few white, unpainted areas helps to dramatize the blacks and bright colors.

Cleanup of materials: Cooking oil removes ink from all surfaces. I like to use a single-edge razor blade to remove the ink from the plexiglass before squirting it with oil to finish cleaning it. Unless you pay for a laundry service to clean your supplies, it's best to use paper towels, as washing oil-soaked rags isn't good for your home washing machine, and putting them in your dryer can cause a fire.

Copper is the most common material for etching plates. After the etching process is complete, the plate is inked and wiped so that the only ink remaining on the plate is caught in the incised lines. Next, damp paper is laid on the plate, and finally the plate and paper are run through a press with a fairly tight pressure setting. The paper picks up the ink that remains in the incised lines. I love the precision that I can achieve with etching—the crispness of leaf shapes and trunk outlines. Although etching materials and techniques are a bit more complex than sketching, watercolor, or block printing, they are easily understood once you take a class; see "Resources" to find places you can take classes. After you get the basics in a classroom, consider joining a printmaking cooperative or a studio with a large press on hand, because you need to have access to a press for etching. All the other media I cover in this book can be done by hand at home.

Carving Tools and the Marks They Make

The tools used for making relief prints are called gouges, and they come in different shapes and numbered sizes: U-gouges and V-gouges (both big and small) and square gouges, which cut sharp, 45-degree grooves in the wood, linoleum, or soft rubber blocks. The square gouge is the most effective for creating sharp corners.

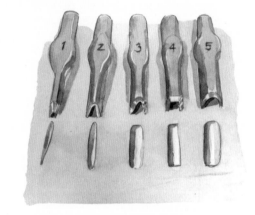

In addition to easily carved rubber blocks, I've worked on wood and linoleum, though I stay away from the latter because it's very hard on the wrist and takes a lot more time. To color the prints, I've used both oil-based inks and watercolors in the Japanese *moku hanga* (*moku* means "wood"; *hanga,* "print") style, which typically relies on water-based media. Because I've produced so many relief prints over the years for calendars and note cards, the easily carved rubber blocks have been my mainstay—I've probably made more than seventy-five prints that way. There's always some new subject I want to try, and if I work

only in the more labor-intensive media, such as woodblocks and etchings, I'll never get to experiment with new designs and new trees.

MOUNTAIN HEMLOCK ALONG THE PACIFIC CREST TRAIL NEAR STEVENS PASS (ETCHING)

Northern Coastal & Cascade Forests

mountain hemlock

shore pine

lodgepole pine

grand fir

western white pine

Pacific yew

Pacific rhododendron

Oregon grape

skunk cabbage

salal

devil's club

western sword fern

Townsend's chipmunk

varied thrush

pileated woodpecker

Pacific tree frog

Cascades frog

rubber boa

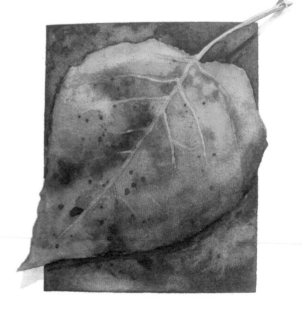

But a dead tree may be as arresting, as filled with personality, in death as it is in life. Even in its final moments, when the massive trunk lies prone and it has moldered into a ridge covered with mosses and fungi, it arrives at a fitting and noble end. It enriches and refreshes the earth. And later, as part of other green and growing things, it rises again.

—Edwin Way Teale, *Dune Boy: The Early Years of a Naturalist*

The forests of the coastal areas of the Pacific Northwest are among the most beautiful in the world. Absent are grand panoramic vistas; instead, the gaze is directed heavenwards to the tops of two-hundred-foot tall Douglas-firs and western redcedars. And the view is not complete without a scan of the forest floor, littered with hundreds of fallen trees, rotting logs, fungi, lichens, mosses, and sword ferns. These forests are known as temperate rainforests, but a more apt term would be moist forests, since a tropical rainforest gets rain all year, whereas our Northwest forests experience a rainy season in winter and a dry season in summer. Some coastal forests contain greater biomass than tropical rainforests, due to the immense height and girth of the giant trees that thrive here. Both types of forest gather nutrients through mycorrhizal underground networks, but the two ecosystems diverge in many ways, including the number of species present in each zone. In Olympic National Park in Washington State, for example, there are as few as 12 tree species. In a comparable acreage in the tropics there may be as many as 120 types of tree. It also takes much longer for the fallen trees in a Northwest forest to decompose because of the cooler temperatures, so there is a lot more litter on their floors than is found in tropical forests.

The dry summers of the Pacific Northwest favor conifers. The leaves of deciduous trees, with their large surface area, suffer without adequate summer moisture. The wax-coated conifer needles are protected from the dry conditions by going somewhat dormant in summer; they become active again during autumn and spring, and even in winter, if temperatures are above freezing, as they maintain their foliage year-round. Since they lose only a small fraction of their oldest needles during fall, they don't require as many nutrients to produce fresh growth as a deciduous tree does, as it must leaf out fully each spring.

There is a spare beauty to the temperate rainforests because of the uniformity of species, something I appreciate greatly as an artist. These forests have been compared countless times to cathedrals, and with good reason. The immense tree trunks are like the piers supporting the ceiling vaults of a Gothic church; when you walk on a trail, or sit and sketch a forest where there are a number of old growth trees together, it is much like experiencing the calm you might feel processing down the nave of a cathedral.

Among the loveliest companion species found in the coastal forests is Pacific rhododendron. The first time I saw one in the Oregon Cascades I was stunned—feeling, as I often do in the wild, that there is nothing in a garden to compare to the effect of seeing a garden favorite growing wild. Trillium is another favorite here, beautiful in all seasons but especially in spring, when its three-part white flowers carpet the forest floor. Old-man's beard lichen is completely surprising, too, draped from tree branches in the moistest forests. Douglas squirrels, with their richly colored gold-orange bellies, are also common and quite distinct from the common gray squirrels of urban areas.

Western redcedar *(Thuja plicata)*

This colonnade of cedars (below and opposite) grows just outside Newhalem, Washington, in North Cascades National Park. I have visited them many times on the Trail of the Cedars, sometimes on my own, and at other times with students from the North Cascades Institute so that they can sketch and appreciate them with me. During the wildfires of 2015, the flames leapt down the ridge all the way to the trail and it was closed for a time. Fortunately the fire never reached the cedars, but above them you can still see the blackened forest as it extends up to the ridgetop.

STELLER'S JAY

The colonnade reminded me of the extensive arcades that I saw in Bologna, Italy. The entire city is filled with beautiful archways and pillars and covered porticos. These cedars grew so regularly because they started their lives as seedlings on a nurse log and found conditions so ideal that they all matured relatively at the same time. When I admire something in nature this much, I am often tempted to try to represent them again and again in different mediums.

Western redcedars grow from Alaska to as far south as the fog belt that stretches from southern Oregon to Monterey County in California. They are also found in the Rocky Mountains in western Montana, up to 3,000 feet in the north and up to 7,000 feet in the south. As timber it has always been highly valued because of its rot resistance and fragrance. Lewis and Clark knew they needed to find a tree large enough to build watercraft for their westward journey downriver to the Pacific, and they were fortunate to discover the cedar in Idaho, where they created four large pirogues, plus one smaller one for scouting.

The tree's beautiful foliage is scalelike and drapes from the drooping branches. It is extremely fragrant and resinous. The cones are small, only about half an inch long. The trunks are encased in a rich reddish-brown bark that is stringy. The base of very mature trees can be buttressed and ridged with deep furrows. Trees can grow up to 175 feet, and trunk diameters can reach 8 feet, the second widest trunk among the world's tree species.

While American Indians used these trees extensively, they did not fell many because they were able to cut planks and harvest the bark and the roots without substantively injuring the trees. Baskets, ropes, and mats were made from the stringy bark. Native people in southcentral Washington State used the cedar roots for coil-style baskets, once the outer covering, or "skin" as they called it, was stripped. They separated the roots into three bundles: the skin to be dyed for decoration, the rougher pieces for the coil foundation, and the long smooth pieces for the stitching materials.

I saw these beautiful living trees and the fallen cedar at Ohanapecosh, site of the famous old growth Grove of the Patriarchs within Mount Rainier National Park.

WESTERN REDCEDARS, GROVE OF THE PATRIARCHS, MOUNT RAINIER NATIONAL PARK

TECHNIQUE
Watercolor Crayons

For this sketch I used a hot press watercolor paper with some intensely pigmented watercolor crayons. I lightly drew in the main contours with a graphite pencil before adding the colored crayons, beginning with the lightest values. It's important to draw lines in the direction of the contours of the tree trunks; that way, you indicate the beautiful, ridged texture of the redcedar trunk. I also added greens for the ferns.

Next I applied water with a clean brush, gently brushing it in the same direction as the crayon strokes; this helps to create broader areas of color. When using crayons I make sure to leave some whites. Solidly filling in everything can create too much opacity. The last step is to add the darkest marks, and most of the time I don't add water to those. I let them create the edges without blurring or making them indistinct.

CEDARS ALONG THE CARBON RIVER, MOUNT RAINIER NATIONAL PARK

Sitka spruce *(Picea sitchensis)*

The Sitka spruce is present in all coastal areas of the Pacific Northwest and is the dominant tree species along the Oregon coast. Everywhere are enormous, buttressed trunks, clothed in a rough-textured bark without furrow or grooves. The color ranges from gray violet to maroon and cinnamon, hues often overtaken by the bright chartreuse of mosses and other epiphytes. In young trees the branches reach up toward the sky, uplifted in a herringbone pattern, but in much older individuals, many branches have been weighed down, so that they jut out at nearly a 45-degree angle. The flat needles are ⅝ to 1 inch long, and bright yellow green on the upper surfaces and blue green and waxy beneath. The cones are 2 to 3½ inches long, cylindrical, and orange brown.

Artists look for underlying patterns, setting aside the extraneous to penetrate to the fundamental order in a landscape. In the coastal forest, with such limited numbers of tree species, the organization is obvious. The landscape is remarkably uncluttered and simple because of the dominance of the spruce—it punctuates all the vertical and horizontal space like a musical score, tall trunks and perpendicular branches at regular intervals.

The branches of this king of Spruces have an upward sweep suggestive of strength and rejoicing; from these the branchlets hang down in a beautiful weeping habit . . . the young tree, and the trees by the side of the highway with room to expand, are clothed to the base in thick-set numberless boughs. The ancients of the deep woods, on the contrary, have tall bare trunks—and what trunks!

—Donald Culross Peattie, *A Natural History of Western Trees*

SITKA SPRUCE AND WESTERN REDCEDAR ON LAKE SERENE TRAIL, WASHINGTON

DEER AT CASCADE HEAD FOREST, OREGON

In the mornings when I teach at Sitka Center for Art and Ecology, on the central Oregon coast, I like to get up early and walk down to the Salmon River Estuary, which sits below the campus. I often encounter does and their young fawns. On a sunny morning in July or August, the sunbeams penetrate the cool mist and illuminate the spruce, maple, and alder trunks, as well as the mahonia and sword fern fronds. Painting this Sitka spruce forest (opposite) in the morning light was challenging, as the mist made certain elements very hazy, whereas others were more clearly delineated. To do it, I had to work on different parts of the watercolor at different times. When I have a subject like that, I try to divide the landscape into quadrants, wetting each quadrant a little bit beyond its perimeter so that I don't end up with hard edges between the four quarters.

In July 2020, I wrote in my journal:

I was heading west back across the Cascades on Highway 2 on a Saturday afternoon in July, a warm day, but sunny and beautiful. The highway is just two lanes, one in each direction, and is often slow, especially on weekends.

Nearing Eagle Falls the traffic came to a dead stop. After about five minutes of idling we all turned off our engines. The heavily forested valley and steep curves made it impossible to see what was going on, so people started getting out of their cars and walking ahead to find out.

I felt my usual panic over being trapped in gridlock. But then I looked up past the columns of gawkers and noticed the bigleaf maples and alders in their rich summer greens, leaves fluttering gently. I could even hear the river with my window closed. Above the trees I saw the dark Gothic form of Mount Index towering above to the south.

I began to indulge in memories of all the times I had hiked up to Lake Serene on Mount Index. In my early twenties I remember seeing a miner's cabin and I wrote a poem about it. The line "sweetish mash of maple leaves" floated through my mind, which was about all I could remember of the poem. I've always loved the smell of maples leaves and even had a friend give me a jar of honey made by bees whose hive was close by maples. The honey tasted exactly like the fragrance of those leaves. There was the time we hiked there with our son when he was recovering from a major illness. Then I remembered a photo I had taken of my husband standing about one hundred feet below me, beside a massive hemlock that totally dwarfed him.

And the most beautiful memory of all was the place above most of the deciduous trees where a western redcedar and Sitka spruce grew close by on either side of the trail, their roots creating a steep step, the riser of it almost too high for the average leg to step up. And the first time I saw it, two older men in their seventies were talking about these trees. I was impressed by their stamina, hiking this steep trail. And then I was even more intrigued by the attention they were giving these trees. I didn't ask them, but maybe they were botanists, or foresters. They told me what we were looking at. And without those two men and their curiosity perhaps I would not have realized that the Sitka spruce was a rare inland relict. Sitka spruces used to be widespread in the valleys of Puget Sound, extending into the mountains in some cases. Logging took away most of those trees, priceless to the timber industry. So here cedar and Sitka spruce were joined in a mountain embrace that must have been much more common in the days before logging.

SITKA SPRUCE

Coastal Survivors

Coastal trees are exposed to many stresses, many quite similar to those impacting timberline trees (see the "Timberline Survivors" sidebar in Subalpine Forests). Coastal stresses include wind, storms, salt water, and salt spray. Sitka spruce along cliffs and headlands have a different shape altogether from the trees that grow just one hundred feet inland. In my sketchbook I painted a Sitka spruce that I saw on the Washington Coast at Cape Disappointment.

Shown below is my sketch of a Douglas-fir at Rosario Beach near Deception Pass, its growth habit completely unlike the "normal" Douglas-fir. Yet another Douglas-fir on Lopez Island is flagged (with branches only near the top of the tree) and the trunk is canted leeward. Shore pines are genetically the same as lodgepole pines and often form picturesque shapes along the coast, much like the Douglas-firs.

SITKA SPRUCE AT CAPE DISAPPOINTMENT, WASHINGTON

DOUGLAS-FIR, LOPEZ ISLAND, WASHINGTON

Douglas-fir *(Pseudotsuga menziesii)*

In Mount Rainier National Park's Grove of the Patriarchs, there are trees that have survived over one thousand years. Among the most notable are the twin Douglas-firs (opposite), which I sketched in honor of my twin sister, Jane. The grove, situated on an island in the Ohanapecosh River, survived numerous catastrophic fires in the area because the water protected it from the encroaching flames.

There are two varieties of Douglas-fir: the taller and faster-growing coastal Douglas-fir (*Pseudotsuga menziesii* variety *menziesii*) and the shorter, slower-growing and more cold-tolerant inland or Rocky Mountain Douglas-fir (*Pseudotsuga menziesii* variety *glauca*), which I write about in the Rocky Mountain Forests chapter. Habitats can change the growth habits of these trees, though, and you might find a wind-exposed coastal tree that is stunted, and an inland tree in a wet ravine that is very tall.

The needles are about an inch long and encircle all sides of the branchlets. Unlike spruce they are not stiff. The cones are unique and easily identify the tree when they lie on the ground beneath it. Each scale of the cone has a three-part seed tucked under it, and those seeds have been described as the back legs and tail of a mouse.

Jerry Franklin, Forest Scientist

University of Washington forestry professor Jerry Franklin graduated from Oregon State University's School of Forestry during the height of the logging that was used for housing for returning World War II veterans. He always knew he wanted a career focused on protecting forests and trees. In 1981, he was the lead author on a paper called "Ecological characteristics of old-growth Douglas-fir forests," the purpose of which was to document these forests and ecosystems before they were completely cut down. In 1994, forest practices changed as a result of the Endangered Species Act and the Northwest Forest Plan, which focused on maintaining biodiversity and protecting older forests and the species, such as the spotted owl, that relied on them. Franklin has continued to research trees and forests during his long career and to advocate for forestry practices that encourage letting older trees grow larger before harvest—not only the classic colossal old growth species, but even younger plantation trees. He believes that forests should not be stripped down to nothing, because when other plants are preserved, forests are able to recover both from the removal of trees and from drought, fire, insects, and many of the challenges they face from a warming climate. The entire forest is important, all parts of it—the soil, open areas, saplings, canopy, understory, and dead and dying trees.

The bark of a young Douglas-fir is smooth and gray, but after decades the bark becomes very thick. Trees that are more than one hundred years in age have deeply furrowed, cinnamon-gray-brown bark. Often they are covered with beautiful lichens in many different colors, depending on the location. Some are bright yellow green; perhaps the most exquisite are the celadon-hued lichens that can cover most of the trunk. In very old trees the bark can be as thick as six inches, which protects the inner tissue from fire.

Coastal Douglas-firs have a wide range, from just south of the southeastern tip of Alaska to about one hundred miles south of San Francisco. Farther inland they grow from the Cascades of Washington in the north to as far south as Yosemite National Park. Douglas-firs are the second tallest trees in the world (after the redwoods). The tallest living Douglas-fir, the Doerner Fir in Coos County, Oregon, is 327 feet tall. Some of the largest specimens have trunk diameters over twelve feet.

Spotted owls and red tree voles live in old Douglas-fir trees, as does the marbled murrelet. Mule deer browse the lower branches of Douglas-firs in winter, causing the trees to look as if they had been pruned.

Douglas-fir is not shade-tolerant, so they tend to be overtaken (or succeeded) by grand fir, western redcedar, western hemlock, Engelmann spruce, and subalpine fir.

DOUGLAS-FIR AND DOGWOOD

TECHNIQUE
Douglas-fir Drybrush

I began this watercolor with a thin glaze of color, moving between pale blue and yellow green. Once that dried I painted the tree trunk, leaving some areas of the glaze untouched, in order to give a sense of light hitting the trunk. The key to using the drybrush technique is to blot the brush on a towel before dragging it across whatever area you are trying to add texture to. If there is too much paint on the brush it will simply lay down a smooth, unbroken wash, and what you are trying to achieve is a broken wash with many areas left unpainted. It's a good idea to try this out first on a piece of scratch paper. I still do that after so many years of painting because I am never sure whether my brush is too loaded or not. It is much better to have it drier than too loaded with paint. It is always such a joy to encounter an old survivor in the forest, like this tree, perhaps as old as seven hundred years. I found it along the Shadow of the Sentinels Trail, just off the Baker Lake Road and close to Highway 20. It's an easy half-mile level walk. I painted the background plant life with a little less care than the fir. The vine maples surrounded it, as they so often do in a coastal or lower elevation Cascades forest, and the bright splash of their leaves only enhanced my impression of the solidity and grave presence of the old tree.

Bigleaf maple *(Acer macrophyllum)*

Bigleaf maples range from southwestern British Columbia to Southern California, at elevations of up to 1,000 feet in northern areas and up to 5,500 feet in the south. The tree can grow as large as seventy feet tall and live up to two hundred years, and has a broad, rounded crown with branches that sometimes droop. (Trees in the southern latitudes are much smaller.) As its name suggests, the bigleaf has enormous leaves, sometimes as wide as twelve inches and up to ten inches long. There are five pointed lobes on the leaves, which are a medium green on top and paler and a bit hairy beneath. Leaves turn a rich gold in autumn. In spring the male and female flowers hang in drooping clusters from the ends of the twigs, and the seeds, known as samaras and popularly referred to as helicopters, are 1 to 1½ inch long. Their aerodynamic shape helps them drift down. The dispersal methods of trees and plants inspired some early airplanes and other aircraft—the Museum of Flight in Seattle has a plane from the World War I era that has samaralike wings. Northwest Coast Indians used the wood of this maple for canoe paddles.

The bigleaf maple is beautiful in all seasons, and there are many places to see them, both in the wild and in city parks. There is a spectacularly large one on the loop trail at Discovery Park in Seattle.

A mature bigleaf maple in winter in the Pacific Northwest looks like a giant sponge, with mosses growing on anything even close to a ledgelike surface. This tree in Olympic National Park (opposite) presides over other much smaller trees and ferns. You can't walk past it without admiring its girth and height and the mosses and epiphytes brightening its dark, almost Gothic presence.

BIGLEAF MAPLE, YOSEMITE

Vine maple *(Acer circinatum)*

This small, elegant tree grows from southwestern British Columbia to as far south as Northern California; another similar maple—the Douglas or Rocky Mountain maple (*Acer glabrum*)—grows in the Rockies. Height can be up to twenty-five feet, with a trunk diameter of up to eight inches, but for the most part, all the branches and trunks are thin, reminding me of the hybrids in a Japanese garden.

Vine maple leaves are opposite and 2½ to 4½ inches wide with long, pointed lobes. Colors are remarkable in all seasons. In early spring the bright chartreuse of their new growth is startling. In autumn they range from gold to orange to scarlet and crimson.

Vine maples grow in moist areas along streams and in the shade of conifers, and are also found in avalanche chutes on mountainsides where they can appear to be flowing down like flames. Two places where I have seen that phenomenon are Mount Rainier National Park and Tumwater Canyon along the Wenatchee River just west of Leavenworth, Washington.

I painted this watercolor of a lone vine maple growing beside Diablo Lake (opposite) because I was so taken with the complementary hues of the maple and the lake. In order to create those very thin branches, I used a rigger brush, which is so named because it was used by artists to paint the very thin lines of a ship's rigging. I painted the twigs after the wash that I had laid for the lake was dry. You can paint directly on top of a previous wash if the color is darker and the wash is completely dry.

On another visit to the North Cascades I saw vine maples alternating with birches and alders in deep forest. I made a quick sketch of it with my class, and then later used that sketch to create the etching (opposite). The etching is done with a mixture of ultramarine blue and soft black ink, which creates the blue-black color of the trunk and leaf outlines. Then when the ink is dry, I hand tint with watercolor, beginning with the brightest lightest yellows and golds.

The Romance of the Old Growth Forest

We live entirely, especially if we are writers, by the imposition of a narrative line upon disparate images, by the "ideas" with which we have learned to freeze the shifting phantasmagoria which is our actual experience.

—**Joan Didion,** *Essays and Conversations*

One late spring day several years ago I hiked up McClellan Butte near Snoqualmie Pass, about an hour from Seattle. This popular trail begins with a jam of alders, bigleaf maples, salmonberries, and other plants common to lower-elevation mountain sites. It's sunny, cheerful, and a little chaotic because all the bigger conifers are still struggling to gain a foothold. The out-of-print hiking guide I used made no mention of older specimens. So I was overwhelmed when I reached a bench, about a third of the way up the trail, crowded by old growth trees. I wrote about it afterwards, and described a grove full of magic: "Huge trunks of towering Douglas-firs and mountain hemlocks surrounded me, their delicate branches high above sending traceries of light downwards. . . . The giant trees created an enclosed and charmed place."

More recently I returned to the trail and perceived something entirely different. The bench I had written about was very small, and the trees grew mostly along a slope. The "old growth" was patchy, maybe ten or twelve Douglas-firs and hemlocks spread out over a couple of acres, with cedars remaining only as stumps and snags. The reality of this place was so much more complicated than my earlier memory—the one that created an alternate world with an intact old-growth ecosystem. Instead I found a messy ecosystem—with no clear delineation between virgin forest and upstart species—this time I admired both the survivors and the other plants that surrounded them. This was not Romantic untouched nature. And it made me aware that even an old-growth forest, whether in the Pacific Northwest, or in Yosemite, or in a redwood grove along the California coast, is a place where change is happening all the time. Trees have life spans, and they fall and decay. New trees are growing, too, all the time, to replace the ancients.

TECHNIQUE
Tinted Paper and Etching

The first time I tried this image, I settled on one of my favorite mediums: watercolor. I chose a Strathmore watercolor paper (these come in various tints) in pastel blue for the maple woods because I saw the blue as the underlying hue of the maple trunk and lighter twigs and also the background sky. There is no color on those areas—it is just the blue of the paper that makes it look as if it is gray or painted soft blue. Next I painted the gold areas and the burnt sienna colors, and then did the background neutral browns. The last step was adding the darker hues, of which there are not too many—see the area on the lower left behind the lighter trees.

I liked the image enough to try it as an etching, and I have done it using both white and blue Rives BFK paper, though my preference is blue. The etching doesn't capture the texture of the trunk as well as the watercolor, as the tooth on the watercolor paper breaks up the color enough to make the trunk look more realistic. Still, utter realism is never what we are after as artists—we look instead to express how a tree affects us, and that can happen in multiple mediums, or in one, in many different ways.

BIGLEAF MAPLE TRUNK IN A WOOD

MAPLE WOODS

Black cottonwood *(Populus balsamifera)*

Black cottonwoods can grow up to 150 feet tall, especially where there is adequate moisture, as in the Columbia River drainage. They are common in the Pacific Northwest from Alaska to Baja California as well as in the Rockies in Alberta, Montana, and Idaho. They are most successful on moist or gravelly soils in valleys, streambanks, and floodplains, so strictly speaking they are riparian (wetland) trees rather than coastal forest or montane trees. They require sunshine, and if they are shaded, other species will crowd them out.

On young trees the bark is smooth and gray or sometimes a brownish yellow. On older trees the bark is thick and ridged and richly textured with deep furrows. The leaves are toothed, three to six inches long, two to four inches wide, and slightly triangular. Reddish-purple male and female catkins (flowering spikes that hang down on many trees, like willows, hazels, and alders, as well as cottonwoods) form on separate trees in springtime, and the fruits are borne in capsules that break open in early summer. Often a trail or sidewalk will collect large drifts of the "cotton," looking exactly like snow.

Throughout the West, cottonwoods are in their glory in fall. There is nothing to compare to the sight of them beaming their golden light alongside riverbanks or playing against the cool-hued conifers on western slopes, as seen in my watercolor of the lone cottonwood on the Wenatchee River (page 60). On the east slopes of the Cascades the gold illuminates the more olive-hued pines and desert landscapes.

BLACK COTTONWOODS

YOUNG COTTONWOODS

TECHNIQUE
Mist

In order to paint mist in watercolor, take advantage of the medium's greatest asset: the ability to work on wet paper! My first step in painting the Wenatchee River cottonwood was getting the whole area of forested slopes wet with clear water, as well as the area for the cottonwood tree. Next I painted the bright gold of the cottonwood tree and then the blue of the conifers, all this very quickly while the paper was still wet. When adding paint to the wet paper it's important not to load the brush up too much with water; be sure to use a fairly saturated paint as the wet paper will always dilute your paint. Plus if the brush has too much water, you will end up with a backrun, or bloom—a big splotch of water in the middle of the color.

In the first stages of painting I sometimes use my ¾" flat brush so I can get the paint on quickly. Then, as you get the paper covered in color, begin to add much more saturated paint of the same hue, or you can vary the hues a bit, with a smaller flat brush, making sure to keep your brush perpendicular to the paper. These short, vertical lines will suggest conifer shapes—a very fast way to fill up an entire mountainside when you are working wet into wet. If you wait too long, the lines will simply be hard edges and won't spread out on the wet paper—the spreading paint is a neat trick that indicates the horizontal branches of a conifer.

COTTONWOOD ALONG THE WENATCHEE RIVER

Nature holds the beautiful, for the artist who has the insight to extract it. Thus, beauty lies even in humble ... things, and the ideal, which bypasses or improves on nature, may not be truly beautiful in the end.

—Albrecht Durer, in a letter to theologian Philip Melanchthon

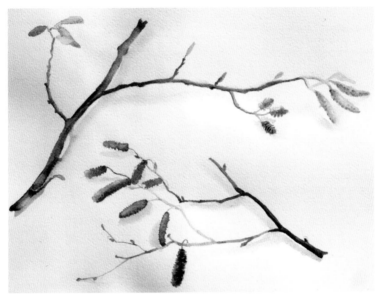

ALDER CATKINS

Red alder *(Alnus rubra)*

Alders grow up to one hundred feet tall and range from southeast Alaska all the way to central California, and from the Pacific coast to as far east as northern Idaho, up to 2,500 feet in elevation. The bark of the trunk is unmistakable: gray to white, smooth, and almost always speckled with lichen patches. The slightly toothed oval leaves are 3 to 6 inches long and 1½ to 3 inches wide. Male flowers are yellow drooping catkins 4 to 6 inches long. The narrow, reddish female flowers are ⅜ to ½ inch long. The alder grows in moist soils, in gravel, sand, and clay, and is common along streams and on lower mountain slopes. They are happy in a wide variety of locations, including the Cascades. In many foothills and lowland forests of the Pacific Northwest, alders are the first trees to return after fire or logging.

I like alders best in winter, when the understory has mostly gone dormant and all you see are the endless columns of the alder trunks, lichen-dappled, moss-dressed, sometimes even brighter than the sky when it is dark and overcast. On a December day in the foothills near Seattle, walking into the sun southward and nearly blinded, all you can see are penumbras of emerald-green moss along the vertical edges of the trunks. Hiking north, the trunks are almost as pale as birches, even though more texture is visible; in fact, they are members of the same family, Betulaceae.

we then used pens and antelope brown FW acrylic ink after drawing quickly in pencil in 30 degree cold.

ALDER AND DOUGLAS-FIR

From a winter entry in my journal:

> *The Cougar Mountain trail offers a swirl of living things, all with their own purposes. Cottonwoods with boles laddering up the trunks, mosses atop each rung, alders patched with creamy lichens, the occasional old conifer: western hemlock, western redcedar, and Douglas-fir. Then there are bigleaf maples and vine maples, their browning leaves now covering the earth of the forest floor. Old-man's beard hangs in delicate chalk-colored green threads from branches. Shelf fungi climb rotted stumps and snags. The day is windy, and the rush of the air through the branches sounds like ocean breakers. . . .*
>
> *Each time I have been here the skies were overcast, sometimes light rain fell. Until yesterday, when sun shone and the sky was an utterly clear deep blue, a rare December event. Through the bare upper branches of maples and alders you could see the blue. The sun's solstice angle is so low here at 47 degrees north that I was blinded when the trail looped back to the south. The lightstruck margins of the mosses were chartreuse green and almost as bright as the sunlight. If there were such a thing as green fire, these trees would be aflame. Steeply canted shadows from the alder trunks advanced toward us on the trail.*
>
> *It occurred to me later that all the greens of the missing alder and maple leaves had been replaced with lichens and mosses and that they were equally bright, speaking of a living season in this season so associated with death and decay. But that was much later. While I was there I only felt the rhythm of my breath and the quiet sound of my footfalls.*

ALDERS IN WINTER, SNOQUALMIE PASS

Suzanne Simard, Forest Scientist

Beginning with her graduate studies at Oregon State University, Suzanne Simard, currently professor of Forest Ecology at the University of British Columbia, worked on a hunch that underground fungi were intimately connected through tree roots and helped the trees gather what they need to thrive—including, water, carbon, nutrients, and hormones. Typically the resources flow from the oldest and biggest trees to the youngest and smallest. In addition, the chemical alarm signals that one tree generates can also move though the fungi to prepare nearby trees for danger. This network between tree roots and the many different forms of fungi that live underground is called a mycorrhizal network. In her early research, Simard set up an experiment with Douglas-firs and paper birches to see if they were exchanging any carbon. To do this, she injected radioactive carbon dioxide into bags that covered one species, and a stable carbon isotope into bags covering the other species. This way she could see if there was an exchange by analyzing the chemicals in each species. It turned out that in the summer, when the young Douglas-firs were mostly shaded by the birch overstory, the carbon flowed from the birches to the firs. In autumn, when the birches were losing their leaves and the Douglas-firs were still growing, the flow of carbon reversed. This groundbreaking study resulted in Simard being featured in the scientific journal *Nature* in 1997; *Nature* coined the term for her study "The Wood-Wide Web." Simard has since become a celebrity, even appearing as a character in Richard Powers' 2019 Pulitzer Prize–winning novel *The Overstory*. When she was young, Simard thought about becoming a writer; at the age of sixty, she published her book *Finding the Mother Tree*, a memoir about her life of research and her abiding belief that forests are more than simply a collection of individual trees.

WESTERN REDCEDAR   DOUGLAS-FIR   WESTERN HEMLOCK   SHORE PINE

PACIFIC MADRONA, DECEPTION PASS STATE PARK

Pacific madrone *(Arbutus menziesii)*

The madrone, or madrona, is an evergreen tree that grows up to 125 feet tall and is found from British Columbia all the way to Southern California. When mature, this extremely striking tree has reddish-brown bark that darkens before peeling off in scales to reveal the golden, smooth bark beneath; the young branches are a rich red with graceful curves. Small white flowers shaped like bells appear in early spring and are followed in autumn by orange-red berrylike fruits up to half an inch in diameter. The smooth, long leaves are glossy and a rich dark green, with a nearly whitish cast on the undersides. The tree is mostly found in coastal areas near sea level in well-drained sites but can also be found inland in canyons and on higher slopes.

The madrone is common in Seattle, where I live and, when I first moved here, my Seattle-native friends gave me the grand tour of the city's most beautiful neighborhoods. That included Magnolia Bluff, perched above Puget Sound northwest of the downtown area. Madrones grow all along the bluff, but when settlers first saw them they misidentified them as magnolias.

One of my favorite places to see the trees is in the San Juan Islands. I've painted them on Lopez Island in the north Sound and closer to the mainland at Deception Pass State Park. The contrast between their rich orange trunks and the Prussian blue hue of the Sound sets up a complementary vibration of color that has brought me back to these places over and over again so that I can re-experience that sensation.

Paper birch *(Betula papyrifera)*

The nineteenth-century British poet John Clare called the birch the "most beautiful of forest trees—the Lady of the Woods." Paper birch is also known as white birch, or canoe birch, as American Indians used the bark for their canoes. The birch, or Betulaceae, family is one of the most widespread plants of the Boreal Kingdom, which extends across the northern latitudes of Eurasia and North America. In North America it is most widespread in Alaska and Canada but does extend southward to northern Washington, Idaho, and western Montana.

Although mature trunks are a lustrous white, the trunks of saplings are dark. The trees can grow to a height of fifty to seventy feet with diameters from one to two feet. The branches droop slightly, and leaves are toothed and two to four inches long. Male flowers are yellowish and hang down as catkins. The female flowers grow on the same twigs as upright catkins, and small cones mature in the autumn. Fall foliage color is a light yellow. The birch requires moist soils and is happy in locations like the one I painted here (opposite), perched on an embankment above Diablo Lake in North Cascades National Park.

California
Redwood
Forests

western hemlock

Pacific rhododendron

chinquapin

western azalea

evergreen huckleberry

maidenhair fern

Roosevelt elk

pine marten

black-tailed deer

Anna's hummingbird

marbled murrelet

Wilson's warbler

spotted owl

banana slug

Pacific giant salamander

red-bellied newt

Look at the bark of a redwood, and you see moss. If you peer beneath the bits and pieces of the moss, you'll see toads, small insects, a whole host of life that prospers in that miniature environment. A lumberman will look at a forest and see so many board feet of lumber. I see a living city.

—Sylvia Earle, as quoted by Roger Rosenblatt in *Time* magazine

Redwoods are the tallest trees on Earth, though they may not have always been the tallest—at one time there was a Douglas-fir that exceeded four hundred feet in height. Before logging, it is almost certain that the redwoods surpassed the closely related giant sequoias in volume. A mature redwood forest produces the greatest biomass on Earth—more than 1,400 metric tons per acre.

The redwoods live only in a narrow fog belt that is 450 miles long and between 5 and 25 miles wide. Their range extends from fourteen miles north of the California border in Oregon's Chetco River drainage (where there are six small stands) south to the Soda Springs Creek area of the Santa Lucia Range south of Big Sur. There are also a few isolated populations in Napa County around forty-two miles from the Pacific coast. The redwood does not like frost, nor the dryness of areas with low winter rainfall or fog, which accounts for their very narrow range. They grow from sea level to about 3,000 feet in elevation.

Douglas-firs grow in almost every redwood forest, and grand fir and Sitka spruce are common north of Eureka, California. South of there, Pacific yew, western redcedar, California Torreya, and Port Orford cedar are found. Hardwood trees like tanoak and Pacific madrone grow in drier forests, while alder, bigleaf maple, and red alder and willows are frequent companion species near the coast.

Redwood trees generally live between 500 and 750 years, so there are many ancients among the groves. And they are very quick to regenerate—if they are struck by lightning, or brought down by a wind, or burned in a fire, they can sprout new crowns where they were topped or send out sprouts from their roots. By growing rapidly, as much as seven feet in their first year, they can quickly exceed the height of their competitors, such as Douglas-fir, that require openings and more light. Places to see redwood forests include Redwood National and State Parks, Muir Woods National Monument, Henry Cowell Redwoods State Park, Humboldt Redwoods State Park, Montgomery Woods State Natural Reserve, Hendy Woods State Park, and Julia Pfeiffer Burns State Park.

Coast redwood *(Sequoia sempervirens)*

Next to a redwood you will sometimes see an interpretive sign that tells you the age of the individual; the oldest specimens can be 2,000 years old. It is a profound experience. First you recognize the shortness of the human life span—we come and go, while the trees remain. I also think it indicates that the trees may be much more important to the health of the planet than we are—otherwise, why would they persist for centuries?

WILSON'S WARBLER

The redwood's bark is fibrous, ridged, and fissured gray or brown, though younger trees have reddish-brown bark. When mature, there are no limbs for about one hundred feet. Branches sweep upwards in a graceful arc. Compared to the sequoia, found in the Sierra Nevada, the redwood bark is darker and grayer. Redwoods have two kinds of leaves. On the tips of new growth, scalelike leaves are ¼ inch long, pointed, encircling the twigs. But there are also flat needlelike leaves ⅜ to ¾ inch long, dark green above and whitish green beneath, appearing in two rows on older twigs. These rows of leaves are one of the best ways to distinguish between a redwood and a sequoia.

Redwoods have two different strategies for reproducing. The cones, which are brown to reddish brown and ½ to 1⅛ inches in diameter, mature in two seasons. Pollination occurs in winter, with two-winged seeds produced the following autumn that are then blown by the wind throughout the forest. Redwoods can also regenerate by growing out of cut stumps, or from their enormous roots if the trunk dies.

Years ago, driving to a family reunion near the San Francisco Bay Area, our family stopped at Tall Trees Grove in the northern part of Humboldt County. As we walked beneath the trees I had a sense that I had been there before. I couldn't quite figure it out but then realized this very forest was a major location for the Star Wars franchise. Specifically, it is the setting for the scene in *Star Wars, Episode VI: Return of the Jedi* where the Ewoks are being attacked by storm troopers in their forest homes on Endor. I find it delightful that the movie found a real-life location that was as otherworldly and magical as the dreamed-up world of Endor.

I didn't need to understand the hypostatic unity of the Trinity; I just needed to turn my life over to whoever came up with redwood trees.

—**Anne Lamott,** *Plan B: Further Thoughts on Faith*

REDWOOD FOREST, HUMBOLDT REDWOODS STATE PARK

REDWOODS AND RHODODENDRON

Save the Redwoods League

The Save the Redwoods League, established in 1918, helped define the California state parks system and initiated and continued the preservation of land through purchases and political activism. In 1905 about 85 percent of the old growth redwoods had never been logged. By 1960 only 10 percent remained uncut. It was only in 1974 that a law was enacted that prevented members of the California Board of Forestry from having any ties with the forestry industry. Until that time, it was mainly through land purchases that groves were spared. In 1986 the League's acquisitions surpassed one hundred thousand acres across a total of thirty-five sites. And by 2021, that number had risen to two hundred thousand acres. The League, over the course of the twentieth century, helped establish and support sixty-six redwood parks and reserves. Land purchases continue, as well as science-based forest restoration work. The League funds research grants on subjects like ecosystem function, community interaction, rare and threatened species, and the impacts of climate change on the redwoods.

CONIFERS AT TWILIGHT

Western hemlock *(Tsuga heterophylla)*

Western hemlocks are the largest of the hemlocks, with slender, at times fluted, trunks and a narrow crown of short branches, often slightly drooping also with a drooping leader. The needles spread in two rows and are flat and short stalked, a shiny dark green above with two broad whitish bands and indistinct green edges. The bark can be reddish brown to gray brown and becomes deeply furrowed, with scaly ridges, as it matures. The cones are ¾ inch to 1 inch long. The hemlock prefers moist, acid soils in flatter areas and lower mountain slopes, growing in dense stands, or together with Sitka spruce and Douglas-fir in redwood forests. It ranges from southern Alaska all along the Pacific coast to northwestern California but also thrives in the Rocky Mountains in northern Idaho and northwest Montana. Along the coast it can be found up to 2,000 feet, and further inland up to 6,000 feet.

Lessons from a Tree

Seed split. Root sprout. Bud leaf.
Delve deep. Hold fast. Reach far.
Seed. Sway. Bow. Lean. Loom.

Climb high. Stand tall. Last long.
Seed. Thicken. Billow. Shade.
Grain. Ring. Grow. Sow seed.

Whine. Sing. Flicker. Glimmer.
Rise by pluck, child of luck,
lightning-struck survivor.

Weather. Hollow. Glisten. Witness.
Seed again. Remember. Testify. Thicken.
Burn. Bleed. Heal. Seed. Learn. Nest.

Host. Guard. Honor. Savor. Seed again.
Fade. Groan. Sag. Crack. Split. Splinter.
Soften. Slough. Grip. Gather.

Arc. Swish. Sail. Fall. Settle.
Log. Stump. Slump. Sag.
Surrender. Offer. Enrich.

Be duff. Enough.

—Kim Stafford
from *Singer Come from Afar*

SNOWY HEMLOCKS AT SNOQUALMIE PASS, WASHINGTON.

Woodlands

northern

madrone
Pacific dogwood
mountain ash
giant chinquapin
bitter cherry
chokecherry
bunchberry
long-tailed weasel
bobcat
garter snake
Cooper's hawk
American kestrel
turkey vulture
Lewis's woodpecker
violet-green swallow
western bluebird

California

valley oak
tanoak
madrone
California buckeye
California bay laurel
California ground squirrel
bobcat
western fence lizard
acorn woodpecker

California quail
California thrasher
Nuttall's woodpecker
yellow-billed magpie

southwest

Pinyon pine
Utah juniper
emory oak
Arizona white oak
Mexican blue oak
silverleaf oak
gray oak
sagebrush
alderleaf mountain mahogany
wood rat
mountain lion
coyote
bobcat
pronghorn
cottontail
pinyon jay
red-tailed hawk
golden eagle
wild turkey
bushtit
titmouse

Woodlands are found all over the West, in the space between cooler, moister conifer forests and arid grasslands and deserts. They can include denser forests of oak and pine but also more savannalike conditions where grasses grow between widely spaced trees. Woodland trees are smaller than moist forest or riparian or montane trees, and stands can be sparser. Species include oaks, pines, junipers, and many scrub and brush-type plants.

Oak woodlands exist in small pockets in Washington State both west and east of the Cascades and in greater concentrations in Oregon, primarily on the west side. Oaks blanket the foothills, lowlands, and lower mountain slopes in California and New Mexico. In colder areas, like the Colorado Plateau and the Great Basin, pinyon pines predominate instead of oaks. There are overlaps, though. Oaks grow alongside pinyons and junipers in southern Arizona and Southern California, as well as in northeastern California.

The pine woodlands cover much of the west: central California and much of Nevada, Utah, Arizona, New Mexico, and Colorado. Rainfall can be as little as twelve inches per year, and summer daytime highs can top ninety or one hundred degrees. In these areas trees are highly stressed, so the number of species can be quite limited.

Wildfire plays a large role in maintaining these woodlands, as American Indians understood when they set small fires to preserve their hunting and acorn-gathering sites. When fires are suppressed, Douglas-firs and junipers readily take over the more open and sunny stands of oaks and other woodland species. Early foresters were more interested in keeping forests and wildlands intact for timber production; they had little understanding of the ecological importance of fires. So when huge fires occurred in Montana, Idaho, and Washington in 1910 (known as the Big Blowup), fire policy changed radically to preserve forests through total fire suppression. In the 1930s the Civilian Conservation Corps put thousands of men to work building firebreaks and fighting fires.

It wasn't until 1970, when there was a better understanding of how fire supports woodlands, and the larger timber-producing forests, that the Forest Service changed its policy to allow fires to burn in designated wilderness areas. For a time, small fires reduced the amount of wood and debris in the understory, fuel that would otherwise allow fires to burn out of control. But then the devastating 1988 Yellowstone fires changed policy once again.

Today, exurban sprawl in many woodland-dominated areas, like California, Arizona, and New Mexico, is another new factor in determining policy for what is called the wildland-urban interface. In addition to human-caused fires, due to the rising population in wild areas, climate change has created conditions for fiercer fires. Now the Forest Service, along with federal, tribal, state, and local partners, is implementing new strategies: resilient landscapes, fire-adapted communities, and safe and effective wildfire response. With greater understanding of the importance of fire, these new policies take new conditions into account.

Northern Woodlands

Oak woodlands in Washington and Oregon are often the result of unusual circumstances. Before white settlement, American Indians deliberately set fires in the woodlands in order to keep the savannas sunny, conditions that the oaks require. American Indians relied on the oak acorns (known as mast) for food, and also made use of the more open slopes and prairies for hunting bigger game. Without this controlled burning, Douglas-firs creep in and then create too much shade for the oaks. There are efforts underway in various state forests to maintain the savannas by culling the Douglas-firs.

Throughout the West, from Washington to California to as far east as Wyoming and New Mexico, ponderosa pines can be found in woodland areas, along with oaks, as well as in pure stands and in mixed coniferous forests.

Ponderosa pine *(Pinus ponderosa)*

I first became acquainted with the ponderosa pine when traveling east of the Cascades to Leavenworth, Washington. Passing through the dense and dark forested slopes of the western Cascades on Highway 2, often in mist or rain, I suddenly emerged into a sunny climate just east of Stevens Pass. What a different world! The understory is almost absent; instead, you find low grasses that turn green in late spring, then are golden for most of the year, and finally buried under winter snow. You can walk through these woods even without trails, unlike the alpine or coastal forests of the Pacific Northwest. No bushwhacking required!

The pine was named by David Douglas, in honor of its ponderous size and heavy wood. John Muir remarked on the beautiful stands of ponderosa pines in the Sierra Nevada. These open, parklike forests no longer exist because fire suppression has allowed other species to make inroads. More shade-tolerant incense cedar and white fir are now growing where ponderosa pine seedlings once took hold.

PONDEROSA PINE CONE

The tree grows from 60 to 130 feet with trunk diameters of up to four feet. The needles are usually three to a bundle and are stout, stiff, and dark green, from four to eight inches long. The reddish bark is especially beautiful in mature trees, with rough and furrowed ridges and large and flat, scaly plates. If you put your nose up to one of the ridges, you'll smell a scent something like vanilla. The attractive cones are two to six inches long.

Ponderosa pine forests extend from inland British Columbia to as far south as northern Mexico. They are very common in the inland valleys and eastside foothills of Washington, Oregon, and California, as well as Montana, Idaho, and Colorado. Some large western cities are even built within a ponderosa pine forest: Spokane, Bend, Flagstaff. Suburbs of Boise, Colorado Springs, Helena, and Rapid City are also within a pine forest.

Witness Tree

I discovered the Witness Tree, an Oregon white oak, while exploring the vineyards west of Salem, Oregon, on a trip to the Pacific coast where I taught at Sitka Center for Art and Ecology. Oregon white oaks were used in the nineteenth century as survey markers for property boundaries. This tree was a marker for the southeast corner of the Claiborne C. Walker donation land claim, but the original marks incised onto the trunk on July 8, 1854, were carved away and no one knows why. All that remains is a large cavity in the tree. It is a beautiful and stately tree when seen from the foot of one of the picturesque foothills between the valleys and coast range in Oregon.

Oregon white oak *(Quercus garryana)*

When I was a teenager in Minnesota, there were two big oaks that grew right beside my bedroom window. At night the leaves would rustle, creating sounds that were alternately musical and spooky to my young ears. I miss those Great Lakes hardwood forests, but we are not without oaks in the Pacific Northwest, and California has perhaps the most beautiful array of oaks anywhere in the world.

Garry, or Oregon white, oaks have several habits of growth. They sometimes grow as high as seventy feet, but in less benign, drier locations they become shrubby with multiple small trunks. The leaves are an attractive shape with deep lobes, shiny dark green above and a bit lighter and usually hairy beneath. In autumn the leaves can turn a rich gold.

TECHNIQUE
Graphite Pencils

Big Red (near Bend, Oregon) is a champion tree, 167 feet tall, nine feet three inches in diameter, and with a crown spread of sixty-eight feet. Fencing surrounds it, in order to protect it from visitors. Additionally, the Forest Service is thinning trees around Big Red to prevent wildfires from getting too close. It is believed that loggers spared the tree because it had sustained weather damage and wouldn't have brought much value as a lumber specimen.

I decided to start this drawing above the base of the tree and to leave out the other trees in the forest. Although they would have put Big Red in perspective, I wanted this to be a portrait of an individual, rather than a landscape.

I used a range of graphite pencils, starting my drawing with the lightest, an HB. I used a 3B to lay in tone throughout the sketch. In order to emphasize the branching patterns and the delicate twigs, I needed to use a darker pencil. I started with a 6B and progressed to an 8B as I got to the darkest areas.

BIG RED, PONDEROSA PINE

I first saw the shrubby Oregon white oak savannas (above) between Yakima and the Columbia River on Highway 97 in autumn, when the oaks were turning a rusty gold. They used to be more widespread in Washington but are now limited in western Washington to areas near Interstate 5 at Fort Lewis, south of Tacoma. Between Tacoma and Vancouver, Washington, there was once a vast prairie that supported oaks, as noted by William Tolmie, a nineteenth-century plant collector and botanist who worked as a physician for the Hudson's Bay Company. In eastern Washington the oaks grow on the foothills of the Cascades along Highway 97 between Yakima and Goldendale. The tree is much more common in Oregon, and if you visit the wine country west of Salem, the rolling foothills are dotted everywhere with Oregon white oaks.

The second time I saw the oaks on the eastern slope of the Washington Cascades was in May after a very wet winter, and this is what I wrote about that visit:

OAK LEAVES AND ACORN

We walked up the gravel forest service road, and saw no one. It was too early in the year for scout troops and other visitors and the place is not near any larger towns or cities. As we ascended past the deepest forest, we saw golden balsamroot blooming in bright drifts in the open pine forest. In moister draws and gullies, delicate Jeffrey's shooting star flowered. Finally at the top of the road we reached the oak meadow. We knew to expect that and went partly to see the great horned owl that frequents the larger oaks. And of course we wanted to experience the new bright growth of the tiny oak leaves that clustered in the crowns. We were completely surprised by what we saw. Thousands of blue camas lilies covered the broad meadow like a lake of flowers. We walked through this miraculous field as if we were the first people who had ever seen it.

I later learned that an early description of camas flowers came from Meriwether Lewis. On their trip home from the Pacific, he and his party had to wait to cross the Bitterroot Mountains in Montana because the snow was still too deep. At Weippe Prairie, on June 12, 1806, Lewis wrote that the camas were in bloom and "at a short distance it resembles lakes of fine clear water, so complete is this deseption [*sic*] that on first sight I could have swoarn [*sic*] it was water."

More than twenty years later David Douglas observed the same flower and noted its use as a staple by Native peoples in both coastal and plateau cultures. The roots are dug up after the plant has bloomed and is about to go to seed. The tubers are then roasted and dried for use in the winter. Douglas noted the Oregon white oak and was delighted to discover it, as he, like me, had been so enamored of the great hardwood forests of the east and Great Lakes.

OREGON WHITE OAKS AND CAMAS

California Woodlands

Four species of deciduous and four species of evergreen (or live) oaks are native to California. The deciduous oaks are found in California's interior foothills and valleys, where winter is colder and summers drier and hotter. Evergreen oaks tend to live closer to the coast, where winters are milder and conditions are overall moister. The Central Valley is dominated by blue oak and interior live oak. The interior species adapt to summer drought with long taproots and thick leathery leaves, which help prevent moisture loss.

These California woodland ecosystems are frequently less densely packed with trees than other woodlands. Chaparral is more common here, and that includes many low shrubs and grasses that grow between the oaks, like California buckwheat, flannelbush, chamise, silktassel, sumac, and birch-leaf mountain mahogany.

Paleobotanists have surmised that California woodland flora migrated from the Sierra Madre in northwestern Mexico during the middle Miocene period, around 25 million years ago. They call this the Madro-Tertiary geoflora; it replaced the Neotropical geoflora of earlier epochs.

How do we distinguish the oak from the beech ... but by the bounding outline?

—**William Blake,** from Exhibition and Catalogue from 1809

FOOTHILLS NEAR SANTA BARBARA

California Oaks

The oak Latin genus name *Quercus* comes from two Celtic words: *quer* ("fine") and *cuez* ("tree"). Worldwide there are up to five hundred species of oak, with some very different leaf shapes and growth habits, but there are four characteristics common to all of them: their fruit is an acorn, wind-pollinated flowers, strong and complex wood, and the ability to live many decades as a result of the strong wood.

California has twenty species of oak. Some are tall and others are more like shrubs that hug the ground. Some retain their foliage year round, while others lose leaves during winter, and still others during times of drought. Several of the California oaks are able to withstand wind, drought, fire, insects, and disease and can live two hundred to three hundred years, and a few more than six hundred years.

California oaks live in several different habitats. The forest oaks live on upland slopes, both montane and riparian, at higher elevations or along streams and rivers at all elevations. The woodland oaks live in more open and sunlit areas at elevations below the forests, and have less moisture. The savanna (sometimes also known as chaparral) oaks grow far apart from one another across grasslands, the driest and warmest habitat.

These are some of the most notable species:
VALLEY OAKS (*Quercus lobata*) are huge trees up to one hundred feet tall. Before the advent of agricultural clearing in the 1880s, the trees lined the Sacramento River on both sides. Ground water pumping lowered the water table and the old groves are now gone. Nowadays the biggest groves are seen in valleys among the coast ranges. They are deciduous and live from Shasta Lake south to the San Joaquin Valley.

INTERIOR LIVE OAKS (*Quercus wislizeni*) are evergreen and are found on Mount Shasta and in the Sierra northern foothills from 1,000 to 5,000 feet in elevation.

BLACK OAKS (*Quercus kelloggii*) are deciduous and found with Douglas-fir and ponderosa pine from southern Oregon along the Pacific coast to the Sierra Nevada range.

BLUE OAKS (*Quercus douglasii*) are deciduous and are distinguished by their blue-green foliage. In their natural habitat they grow in the valleys of the coast ranges, and the lower western foothills of the Sierra Nevada, and

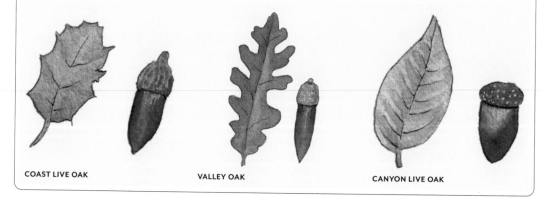

COAST LIVE OAK   VALLEY OAK   CANYON LIVE OAK

BLUE OAK GROVE, CALIFORNIA

the north slope of the San Gabriel Mountains. Blue oak covers about three million acres and is one of the largest ancient forest types in California.

OREGON WHITE OAKS (*Quercus garryana*) are deciduous and found from Washington State down through California's Santa Clara County. They are even found as far north as Vancouver Island in British Columbia.

CANYON LIVE OAKS (*Quercus chrysolepis*) range from Oregon to Baja California and can be found from sea level to 9,000 feet—they have the widest distribution of any oak in California. They are evergreen and assume various shapes, shrubby or tall, depending on location.

CALIFORNIA LIVE OAKS (*Quercus agrifolia*), as evergreens, are perhaps the most picturesque of the oaks and have appealed to the artist in me. The trees often grow low to the ground and have very contorted branches, and at times grow in a miniature size. This oak is confined to coastal areas in central to Southern California. Robert Louis Stevenson found inspiration in California live oaks for his classic novel *Treasure Island.* He wrote that their low branches and the dark recesses created by their foliage and the shadows they cast formed perfect places "under which a murderer might hide." I find them less sinister than Stevenson; my imagination takes me to no such dark places!

Gray pine *(Pinus sabiniana)*

The gray pine is known by several other names: California foothill pine, ghost pine, and bull pine. It grows to a maximum height of about fifty feet and is distinguished by its wispy appearance, with blue-gray foliage delicately topping thin branches and trunks. The drooping needles grow in threes and are eight to twelve inches long. The cones are enormous—six to ten inches long with huge nuts that American Indians prized as a food source. The bark is grayish brown, forming flat plates that look shaggy on older trees. Gray pines grow in small groves or singly on dry rocky sites in foothills and even on valley floors. They are well adapted to drought and can survive on as little as ten inches of rainfall annually. They are most common between 1,000 and 3,000 feet of elevation and are endemic to California. The trees surround the Central Valley, becoming more widespread as you get closer to the Sierra, and also appear in coast ranges.

GRAY PINE, PINNACLES MONUMENT, CALIFORNIA

I first saw a gray pine on a trip to Yosemite. At first glance I thought it was a deciduous tree because of its frail and spindly branches. Some might find it rather homely with its gangly trunk and splayed skeletal branches, scarcely covered at all with foliage, but I found it very graceful and unusual and loved the needles' blue-green color, a glaucous adaptation that no doubt protects it from the heat and extreme aridity.

Gray pines are very common east of Monterey in Pinnacles National Park. On a visit there, I was warned by a ranger against spending too much time under the trees—if a cone falls on you, weighing more than seems possible for a cone, it really hurts. I wanted to collect one, but it's illegal at Pinnacles, so I determined to get one on the highway that leads north toward Hollister. Unfortunately, that highway is one of the narrowest state roads I have ever driven on, and there was no way to stop and pull over to pick one up. Luckily for me, the cones are very popular at holiday time, and many seasonal tree lots sell them, along with other pine cones. I finally managed to buy one a couple of holidays ago and weighed it when I got home: 2.6 pounds. No way would I want that dropping on my head!

Fremont cottonwood *(Populus fremontii)*

The Fremont cottonwood grows to heights of up to eighty feet. The leaves are triangular, like many poplars, with short points and coarse teeth, and turn a rich yellow in autumn. The bark is gray and rough and gets very deep furrows as it ages. The flowers are 2 to 3½ inch catkins, with the males and females on different trees. The tree grows in wet sites and is often found with sycamores, willows, and alders in many different pinyon pine habitats: in deserts, woodlands, and grasslands from Colorado south to Texas and New Mexico along the Rio Grande and from sea level to 6,500 feet in elevation. It's also found in riparian habitats throughout California.

The cottonwoods seen in the watercolor below grew alongside the Merced River in Yosemite Valley. I was so keen to capture a dramatic view of them in autumn, with the granite of El Capitan hovering in a silvery light above, that on that day we got up early so we could see this pure vision in the morning light.

Southwest Woodlands

Woodlands in the Southwest, which include locations in the Great Basin, Colorado Plateau, and Rocky Mountains, are dominated by pinyons, junipers, and several small oaks. Most woodland areas receive only fifteen to twenty-five inches of rain per year, most of which falls between December and March. There is little or no precipitation in summer, and fires occur frequently in these locales.

COLORADO PINYON, BRYCE CANYON NATIONAL PARK

Colorado pinyon *(Pinus edulis)*

The Colorado pinyon, or two-needle pinyon, ranges from Utah and Colorado south to New Mexico and Arizona, growing at elevations from 5,000 to 7,000 feet. It is widespread in open areas, alone or with junipers, on dry foothills, mesas, plateaus, or lower mountain slopes, and is the most common tree in Grand Canyon National Park. The pinyon reaches only fifteen to thirty-five feet in height, and has two needles per bundle. The pine nuts are delicious and a cash crop harvested by American Indians and non-natives and sold to gourmet markets.

Gambel oak *(Quercus gambelii)*

The Gambel oak, also known as the scrub oak, was named for the American naturalist William Gambel (1823–1849). It can be found in most of the southwestern United States, preferring the habitats of canyons, mesas, and mountain slopes, as well as along roadsides. At high altitude, it is the rare deciduous species you will find among ponderosa pines, pinyon pines, and junipers. It typically grows up to twenty to seventy feet, but the Gambel oak is also quite common as a shrub with multiple trunks, forming dense thickets. The bark is thick with rough, scaly plates, and the crown of the tree when it grows tall is rounded. The leaves are classic oak leaves, with five to nine rounded lobes, and are rather leathery, shiny green above and lighter with delicate hairs on the undersides. Gambels can be colorful in fall, either red or yellow. The acorns are ½ to ⅞ inches thick. These oaks range from northern Utah east to southern Wyoming, south to west Texas and southern Arizona and New Mexico, and are very common in the Grand Canyon.

GAMBEL OAK

California Coastal Forests, Chaparral & Scrub

Bishop pine

California live oak

tanoak

California hazelnut

whiteleaf manzanita

chamise

ceanothus

buckbrush

California sagebrush

poison oak

salal

California poppy

beach evening primrose

brush rabbit

northern alligator lizard

lesser goldfinch

golden-crowned sparrow

The immediate coastline of California rarely supports redwoods, which dislike the salt spray and drying winds. Instead, its headlands and dramatic cliffs are home to different species of pine, California live oaks, and chaparral and scrub plant communities. They thrive in the Mediterranean climate, with its hot, dry summers and average rainfall of twenty to thirty inches.

About 9 percent of California's total wildland vegetation is chaparral. Chaparral comes from the Spanish word chaparro, meaning "dwarf oak," and it describes a community of tough, fire-adapted shrubs that frequently grow in dense thickets. Trees are somewhat rare, usually found in ravines or on north-facing slopes, and there is no closed canopy. All of the shrubs have leaves called sclerophylls—tough, leathery, stiff, waxy, and mostly evergreen. Fire contributes greatly to the development of chaparral in California, because the shrubs are adapted to it and need fire to propagate, by sprouting and germinating seeds. Fire also renews the soil, by vaporizing the soil toxins, and the burnt plant material returns nutrients to the soil. Typically these communities burn every ten to forty years, but fire suppression policies changed that, and unfortunately a lot more fuel has developed in the undergrowth, leading to more catastrophic fires. In addition, fewer fires, which the shrubs are able to withstand, mean a larger tree population.

Although they frequently overlap with chaparral, scrub communities are a bit different, often even closer to the ocean and more exposed. Plants include coyote bush, California sagebrush, bush lupine, bush monkeyflower, various grasses, and many other wildflowers. Sand dunes have beautiful flowers like desert verbena and beach evening primrose.

Torrey pine
(Pinus torreyana)

Torrey pine is an unusual tree that is endemic to a very narrow range, concentrated on sea bluffs in only two locations, one a five-mile-wide stretch between the coastal communities of San Diego and Del Mar, and the other on the northeast side of Santa Rosa Island (about twenty-five miles from Santa Barbara). They have always been rare, numbering only about ten thousand trees at present, perhaps due to the fact that they are not able to adequately disperse their seeds. The huge, woody cones open very slowly—sometimes over fifteen years—and then the short seedwing doesn't permit seeds to fly far. The needles are nine inches long and usually in bundles of five—occasionally in three- and four-needled bundles. The tree's preferred habitat is sandy or sandy loam soil from one hundred to five hundred feet above sea level on seaside cliffs and ridges. It is associated with coastal chaparral on the mainland, which includes plants like yucca, agave, and cactus.

TORREY PINE NEAR SAN DIEGO

MONTEREY CYPRESS AT POINT LOBOS STATE NATURAL RESERVE, CALIFORNIA

Monterey cypress *(Cupressus macrocarpa)*

Robert Louis Stevenson wrote, of these cypresses, "No words can give the idea of the contortion of their growth. They might figure without change in a circle of the nether hell as Dante pictured it," but he must have seen the cypresses in winter on a dark and rainy day. When you see them as I did in May, in bright sunshine with teal-colored water behind them, their upper foliage illuminated by the sun, they have nothing of the Inferno in them at all. And yet, even on a fine day there were specimens with lichens and algae that appeared to be either aflame or perhaps in the throes of a mortal end. The shape is unusual, with planar branches jutting out beneath a flat top; in *Conifers of the Pacific Slope*, Michael Edward Kaufmann describes this tree as "charismatic." The Monterey cypress has been celebrated by many artists, including Gunnar Widforss, Armin Hansen, Mary De Neale Morgan, and Carl Oscar Borg.

The Monterey cypress can grow up to eighty feet tall, but it is usually much shorter. Its native habitat is a very small area around Carmel Bay in California. The trees can be grown away from the sea and salt spray and fog, but the result is very unlike the twisted specimens seen along the shore. The bark of the trees begins in youth as a reddish brown but becomes much thicker, grooved, and gray on an old trunk. The scalelike leaves are a bright green, not bluish or glaucous, yet when seen at a distance they can appear quite dark. These cypresses have male and female cones growing on the same tree, and as with junipers and other cypresses, the cones appear berrylike. Long, draping lichen, *Ramalina reticulata*, festoons many of the trees, giving them a ghostly appearance, and often results in the death of the tree. An algae, *Trentepohlia*, coats the ends of branches on some trees at Point Lobos, giving them an orange or red-hued halo. The algae is able to survive out of water because the air is so laden with the moisture of fog and sea spray.

WILDFLOWERS AND GREAT EGRET AT POINT LOBOS STATE NATURAL RESERVE

TECHNIQUE
Iron Gall Ink

For this sketch of coast live oak at Laos Osos State Preserve, I used different saturations of iron gall ink, beginning with a light pencil drawing. Next I brushed a diluted wash of the ink onto the lighter-valued areas of the sketch. As I moved to the darkest trunks and branches I used an undiluted ink and painted it on without adding any water.

Iron gall ink was used for drawing in the Middle Ages and Renaissance. The recipe below has three ingredients: crushed oak galls, ferrous sulphate, and gum arabic. You can also buy the ink from online calligraphy stores. If you make your own, you can harvest the oak

Note: Oak galls are created when a gall wasp lays an egg into a small hole on the underside of an oak leaf. The larva grows, and the tree secretes tannic and gallic acids in response, thus creating the oak gall, also known as a gall nut or oak apple. These are harvested and dried to make the ink. Gum arabic is dried sap from the gum acacia tree and is used as a binder for watercolor. It adds substance to the iron gall ink.

Recipe for iron gall ink, created in 2013 by Andrew Raftery of the Rhode Island School of Design printmaking faculty, based on a 1770 recipe by Luca Cambiaso: Soak 2 ounces of crushed oak galls in 1 pint of water (preferably distilled) overnight, then strain through a cheesecloth into 1 ounce of ferrous sulphate (weigh it on a scale). Add ½ ounce of gum arabic and stir until all is dissolved.

MONTEREY PINE AT POINT LOBOS STATE NATURAL RESERVE

Monterey pine *(Pinus radiata)*

The Monterey pine forms a heavily needled crown dome on a thick trunk. Its bark is fissured and gray brown. Cones are huge, up to six inches long and five inches wide. The needles are bright green, up to six inches long and in groups of three. It grows in limited areas in California and is best known on the Monterey Peninsula and south to Carmel, Pico Creek, Cambria, and Santa Rosa Creek in San Luis Obispo County. It is mostly seen in coastal areas, where it is contorted, or, if seen farther inland in more sheltered areas, it can be leggy.

The tree is very common all over the world in tree plantations, especially New Zealand, where there are over three million acres of Monterey pine. It is the speedy growth and ease of turning the wood into pulp and lumber that make it such a popular plantation tree. If it is grown in a tropical climate it can grow throughout the year and send up twenty-foot-long leaders—the young branches that form each spring. Its genetic variability has been important in creating genotypes selected for rapid growth and easy pollination or cloning. Keeping the wild forms allows scientists to use these forms to breed new genotypes, selected for disease resistance that helps keep timber plantations healthy.

Rocky Mountain Forests

ponderosa pine
lodgepole pine
white fir
blue spruce
grand fir
birchleaf spirea
Pacific ninebark
ironwood
Saskatoon serviceberry
mule deer

white-tailed deer
elk
moose
gray wolf
mountain lion
coyote
lynx
bobcat
grizzly bear
black bear
golden-mantled ground squirrel
marmot
yellow-rumped warbler
song sparrow
western wood-pewee
red-breasted nuthatch
flammulated owl
long-eared owl
red-tailed hawk

SUNSET AT YELLOWSTONE NATIONAL PARK

My frequent trips to Yellowstone National Park made me aware of how each elevation and microclimate of the Rockies has its own attendant species. Low-elevation conifer forests are largely made up of lodgepole pines, which grow back quickly after fires. Ascending, there are more Douglas-firs and Engelmann spruce. In the drier areas there are plentiful Rocky Mountain junipers, which look especially dramatic clinging to the edges of canyons. No Japanese gardener could possibly prune a tree into the fantastic shapes of some of those junipers.

Of all the Rocky Mountain species, the aspens are my favorites, and I have painted them many times. Above Mammoth Hot Springs there is a grove where my students and I once gathered, and also another on the way to Cooke City. Aspens are plentiful in Yellowstone, although somewhat diminished by large elk populations, which favor aspen saplings. The reintroduction of wolves brought the elk population under control, helping to restore some of the groves.

I was powerfully struck by the aspens the first time I saw them in the Lamar Valley in autumn. White trunks against golden autumn grasses, a herd of bison cows and yearling calves a rich umber against brilliant leaves. Then later, on a hike toward Antler Peak in the Gallatin Range, my friends and I saw a small grove, seemingly afloat above Swan Lake. And perhaps the best experience of all was the most recent one: returning to Gardiner from a long drive over Dunraven Pass, we saw sunset on the peaks beyond the Blacktail Plateau, their soft pillowy forms a rose color against the more sober fading yellows of the aspens beside our car.

Western larch *(Larix occidentalis)*

Deciduous larches, also sometimes called tamaracks (although tamaracks are not native to the West), are found in the Rockies, the Alps, and the Himalaya. They are one of the few conifer species that survived the Pleistocene glaciation. Most species couldn't tolerate the severely cold, long winters—this is why the boreal and western mountain forests have such limited species of conifer. (Some conifers were able to escape south to more benign climates: an example is the sequoia in California.)

There are numerous advantages to being deciduous: Larches, which live in nutrient-poor ranges, can store nitrogen in roots and branches when they drop their needles in fall. Their branches, which have no foliage or needles in winter, can bear heavy loads of snow. Their bark is thick and strong and withstands fire and injury.

Their range in western North America includes southeastern British Columbia, the eastern slopes of the Cascades of Washington and Oregon, the Blue and Wallowa Mountains of northern Oregon, the Bitterroots of Montana and Idaho, and the Rockies in Glacier National Park. They grow at elevations of 2,000 to 7,000 feet, depending on longitude. The largest western larch is near Seeley Lake in Montana. It is 153 feet tall and twenty-two feet around the base.

The bark on the trunks of older trees is thick and a beautiful reddish-cinnamon color, deeply ridged. There are fourteen to thirty needles in a cluster, pale green in new growth and golden yellow in autumn. The cones are 1 to 1½ inches long, reddish brown to purple. In A *Natural History of Western Trees*, Donald Culross Peattie describes the fall color thus: "When autumn comes and the sun shines through the golden foliage, the trees gleam for a while like the Aspens in an angelic light."

From my journal:

> In late October, my husband and I visited Shevlin Park, outside of Bend, Oregon. It's a topographic draw, where moisture-loving plants grow protected from the desert environment further upslope. The portal to the larch grove was a small stand of aspens. The aspen leaves were a brilliant gold and the angled light was so intense that even the aspens' normally pristine white bark turned creamy yellow.
>
> After passing through the aspens, we arrived at a wider valley of ponderosa pines and western larches, deciduous conifers that lose their needles each year. Larches turn even more golden than the aspens—the light bounced off the walls of the canyon and transformed the rust brown of the pines into a burnt orange—it wasn't just the larches and aspens—the entire forest glowed.
>
> The quality of the light and the beauty of the place reminded me of the October trip we took to Assisi in Umbria, Italy. St. Francis preached there in the thirteenth century. When he tired of his ardent followers, he walked up Mount Subasio to a cave, the Eremo delle Carceri, which had been used as a hermitage since the early centuries of the Christian church. As Assisi filled up with Franciscan religious folk from around the world, there to celebrate his feast day, we decided to escape the commotion of the town and followed Francis's path up Mount Subasio, in the Apennines, walking through a dark and very closed canopy of holm oak and beech. The entrance to the cave appeared after we emerged from the trees into the bright Italian sunlight. I tried to picture

WESTERN LARCHES NEAR BEND, OREGON

this man, eight hundred years ago, attempting to get away to a place of peace and contemplation. Here it was, in the forest, one small section of a vast limestone cave system known as the karst. The same limestone built all the architecture of the town, a delicate pink-hued rock that turns an unbelievable rose color at sunset, perhaps most especially in late October. It was that same intense emotion arising out of light and color that I experienced in the larch grove.

In Assisi and in the central Oregon larch grove, both times I remember thinking that I didn't want to leave, that I could have stayed there for hours, walking back and forth, if it were possible to somehow drink in that color and have it effect some kind of transformation in me. The gold of a larch grove is a color that only happens in the northern forest at a certain time of year. This is where our Pleistocene ancestors lived, in the north, hunting big animals, gathering plants from the forest, and in a kind of holy exchange with the earth's bounty, painting animals and human hands on cave walls.

Feeling Color Fields

In certain seasons the color fields of western forests summon emotional responses that are impossible to describe. While often what we see provides helpful information, such as the shape of an object, color fields don't necessarily describe objects or tell us anything especially useful about the physical world we are navigating. But they can make us feel so deeply. Is it something like looking at a Mark Rothko painting? You don't really know what the painting means—you only know that it moves you.

Travelers seek out not only the western larch forests, but also the vine maples that flow in flaming color down avalanche chutes, wet forests where bigleaf maple leaves float in autumn golden glory, and moist meadows in the high Rockies gleaming with aspens. Perhaps the best way to understand how these natural color fields affect us is to ask an evolutionary question: Does the pleasure we derive from viewing these natural scenes of light and color help us to achieve the elusive state of flow? The flow that stimulates mental and physical health, slowing heart rate, regulating breathing, all the neurons firing smoothly? What a marvel it is, that well-being brought on by something as simple and pure as color. Artists have perhaps always known about the effect of colors fields, but it is not that selective—it is there for anyone who searches for it.

CASCADES AUTUMN

Rocky Mountain Douglas-fir *(Pseudotsuga menziesii)*

Rocky Mountain or inland Douglas-firs (*Pseudotsuga menziesii* variety *glauca*) are extremely widespread and can be found in forests with western larch, western white pine, western redcedar, white fir, and blue spruce. The needles of the Rocky Mountain Douglas-fir have a slightly different color, leaning toward

TOWNSEND'S CHIPMUNK WITH DOUGLAS-FIR CONE

blue green, rather than the yellow green of the coast firs. The tree is very adaptable and can live where winter temperatures drop as low as minus 70 degrees Fahrenheit, or where summer heat is as high as 110 degrees Fahrenheit. It can live in deserts, moist forests, lava lands, and very cold subalpine elevations. All of this means the Rocky Mountain Douglas-fir has the widest range of any North American conifer in terms of latitude, from northern British Columbia to tropical mountains in southern Mexico. The only place it is noticeably absent is in the basalt-based ponderosa pine forests just west of Spokane, Washington. The populations in southern Mexico may be relicts of what were much more widespread forests of Douglas-fir during the last Ice Age.

Other unique stands of Rocky Mountain Douglas-firs occur at higher elevations, in the mountain grasslands of the Intermountain West. You can see them in Yellowstone National Park at Mammoth, Tower Junction, and along the Lamar Valley. They grow on high ridges and sunny south- and west-facing slopes, above the range of ponderosa pines. As climate change advances, Douglas-firs will most likely recede from southerly Mexican latitudes and extend northward in British Columbia.

I sketched this view high above the Gardiner entrance to Yellowstone National Park on the way to the hamlet of Jardine, Montana. It looks into the Rescue Creek drainage above the Yellowstone River, where Rocky Mountain Douglas-firs grow in the gullies and mountain tops.

RESCUE CREEK DRAINAGE, YELLOWSTONE NATIONAL PARK

it is dark on the Bear Creek Road
and if I had to say why I am still up here
I would say it's because
my car is stuck in snow
and my neighbor's spinning his wheels
trying to pull me out
and another friend has come
to rescue us

but perhaps I'm here
so I may look up
as many times as my neck can stand
to patches of blue night
pierced with white fire-points
in spaces between the conifers
where their bristles
frame the sky
like ragged skylights
opening on galaxies

my mind

flashes star
fir

pulling me back down
but I arch my back
lift my face
to time
flaming above

—**Ilona Popper,** excerpt from
Only Recently We Have Realized

COTTONWOODS AT DECISION POINT, MONTANA

Black cottonwood *(Populus trichocarpa)*

It's fascinating to compare the difference in size between a black cottonwood growing in the riparian land-scapes of the Rockies with one growing in moister climates west of the Cascades—the latter is much grander. See the Northern Coastal and Cascade Forests chapter for detailed information about the cottonwood.

I sketched this view of Decision Point, where Lewis and Clark had to decide which was the correct route to take to the headwaters of the Missouri River. I liked the sketch so much that I wanted to try it again as a studio watercolor. The cottonwoods along the river lend liveliness to the bleached landscape

COTTONWOODS IN MOONLIGHT

and also help to show the river course. From June 3 to June 12, 1805, the Corps of Discovery was faced with a decision. Two rivers joined, one from the north and one from the south, in what is now the state of Montana. They camped on the lower side of the Marias River. The southern river (which turned out to be the Missouri), according to their measurements, was 372 yards across while the northern was 200 yards across. The northern stream (the Marias River) was deeper, though, and looked more like it was the primary stream. In spite of the fact that the other men of the Corps believed that the river from the north was the right route, the two captains were convinced that the southern river was the correct route. Lewis took a few men and headed to the north, and Clark and the rest of the party explored the southern river. In a few days they discovered that the southern route was the right one. Shortly thereafter they confronted the Great Falls of the Missouri, a large obstacle to their progress, which Lewis nevertheless noted for its extreme beauty. They were forced to portage and had to construct wagons to haul their canoes and baggage past the falls.

MISSOURI RIVER COTTONWOODS

iew from Meriwether Picnic Area
Missouri River, Gates of the Mountains

Western white pine *(Pinus monticola)*

The western white pine is quite common in western Montana; I painted this scene showing the pine (on the right) growing beside dramatic cliffs at Gates of the Mountains Wilderness, just outside Helena. The tree can grow to be very large, up to one hundred feet tall, with a diameter of three feet. The needles come five to a bundle and are somewhat thick, with a bluish-green color. The cones are

*This site also commemorat[es]
the 13 smokejumpers who
died in the Mann Gulch fir[e]
Western W. Pine*

brightly

between five and nine inches long, with a somewhat narrow shape compared to other pine cones. These pines prefer moister sites and are often in mixed forests. They range from the northern Rockies in British Columbia south to northwest Montana. They are also found in the Cascades and as far south as the Sierra Nevada all the way to central California. In the north they grow at altitudes up to 3,500 feet, and in the Sierra at 6,000 to 9,800 feet.

Engelmann spruce
(Picea engelmannii)

The Engelmann spruce is a common tree in the West, but only east of the Cascades Crest, and it grows most abundantly in the Rockies as far south as southern Colorado, where pure stands of the tree occur. Its habitat ranges from 2,000 feet in elevation in the north to 12,000 feet in New Mexico. The Engelmann is very shade tolerant, unlike some of its companion species—think of subalpine firs—so it will eventually crowd out all other trees.

The trees have an elegant, attenuated, spirelike shape—they can reach heights of 150 feet—and grayish bark that has small circular plates with violet brown visible around and under the plates. The needles, which are blue green in color, are one inch long, four-angled, and pointed at the tips and can be rolled in the fingers. The cones are up to two inches long. Unfortunately Engelmann spruce are susceptible to bark beetles, so you will encounter groves that have died off.

This lush group surrounded a high mountain lake, and I felt drawn to paint them, with their rich color contrasting slightly with the intense turquoise of the glacial water.

And when the late mountain light begins to leave the summer sky, there is something spirit-like about the enveloping hosts of the Engelmanns.

—Donald Culross Peattie,
A Natural History of Western Trees

Rocky Mountain juniper *(Juniperus scopulorum)*

Rocky Mountain juniper can grow up to fifty feet tall, and many specimens maintain a straight trunk and a narrow, conical crown. The scalelike leaves are opposite, ⅟16 inch long, and can vary from a lovely blueish to a dark green in four rows. The berrylike cones are ¼ inch in diameter and bright blue, becoming a dark blue as they age. A mountain tree, this juniper thrives on rocky soils as well as on limestone and lava outcrops.

Whenever I visit Yellowstone and stay in Gardiner, I like to get up early and hike just inside the park entrance on the Rescue Creek Trail. Nineteenth-century cattle grazing on the Rescue Creek plateau eliminated many trees, but the survivors are especially beautiful. There are several junipers growing beside the Gardner River, and the one on the facing page is one of my favorites; its deeply ridged bark invites touch. I painted this juniper in the early morning light, which makes everything on the trail turn a rich pink.

ROCKY MOUNTAIN JUNIPER, YELLOWSTONE NATIONAL PARK

Quaking aspen *(Populus tremuloides)*

The quaking aspen grows to about fifty or sixty feet with a trunk diameter of about one to one and one-half feet. Bark on a young tree has a greenish hue, but as the tree matures it becomes much whiter, a color broken up by concentric circled ridges and deep brown or black scars. It is easy to misidentify an aspen as a birch or a poplar, especially when the trees are young.

The leaves are simple and slightly toothed, rich green above and paler on the underside. The fall color is a rich gold. In spring, brown catkins, one to two inches long, develop, but seeds don't generally sprout from them. Quaking aspens reproduce themselves clonally, sending out suckers that eventually develop into trees; over time, this results in beautiful, large groves. The tree does not require any particular soil type and can form pure stands at higher altitudes.

The tree's range in North America is very wide, from Alaska east to Newfoundland, and south as far as New Mexico. It can be found from sea level to over 10,000 feet in elevation. The two states with the most aspens are Colorado and Utah. Almost two thirds of all quaking aspens grow on public lands. In the subalpine areas of the Rockies the aspen grows alongside pines at lower elevations and spruce and fir in the higher reaches of its range. In Colorado and in the majority of the southern Rockies, the aspens are generally found in ponderosa pine forests between 6,500 feet and 9,000 feet. As you travel north and ascend in elevation, you are much more likely to see aspens growing on south-facing slopes, where the sun can warm them, whereas in Arizona and New Mexico the trees are most often found on the cooler north-facing slopes. Aspens often populate fire-burned areas, until they are eventually overtaken by conifers. Fossil records prove that aspens have lived in western North America for as long as fifteen million years.

ASPEN AND BISON AT YELLOWSTONE NATIONAL PARK

ASPENS AT YELLOWSTONE NATIONAL PARK

Over the rounded sides of the Rockies, the aspens of autumn,
The aspens of autumn
Like yellow hair of a tigress brindled with pine.

—**D. H. Lawrence,** from *Autumn at Taos*

TECHNIQUE
Dabbing

The easiest way to create the rounded, disclike shape of aspen leaves is to load your brush up with a color and gently dab the paper. You'll end up with small, circular marks, which can be made in different colors if that is called for. While the paint is still wet, you can gently touch it with another color to vary the hues. This technique works for many different types of deciduous trees and is a great help for painting leaves of all colors and seasons.

ASPENS ABOVE MAMMOTH HOT SPRINGS, YELLOWSTONE NATIONAL PARK

Giant Sequoia Groves

white fir

incense cedar

California black oak

ponderosa pine

manzanita

bitter cherry

bracken fern

lodgepole chipmunk

Townsend's chipmunk

mule deer

ensatina

Pacific tree frog

white-headed woodpecker

American robin

warbling vireo

You are yourself a Sequoia. . . . Stop and get acquainted with your big brethren.

—John Muir to Ralph Waldo Emerson on Emerson's visit to Yosemite, May 1871, from *Our National Parks*

The giant sequoia and the coast redwood are closely related, but they live in distinctly different environments and are shaped and grow in unique ways. The giant sequoia has scalelike foliage; the redwood has needles growing in two rows, like a hemlock. The giant sequoia is the largest tree in the world because of the volume of its trunk, whereas the redwood is the world's tallest tree, with a somewhat slenderer trunk profile. The sequoia cones are three times the size of those of the redwood. Yet another difference: the sequoia's wood is much coarser in texture than the redwood's, which has always been prized for its durability—think of ever-popular redwood outdoor furniture.

At one time in Earth's history sequoias lived from Alaska through the Midwest, and from Greenland through Europe and Asia. Today the sequoia is a relict species, with groves in seventy-five locations throughout the central and southern Sierra Nevada. Sequoias require a habitat with deep, moist, unglaciated soil at elevations between 4,500 and 8,400 feet; they are found along the western slope of the Sierra at 4,500 to 7,500 feet, and are protected in Yosemite, Sequoia, and Kings Canyon national parks. The Mariposa Grove in Yosemite is one of the best places to see the giant sequoia, and some of the champion individuals live here as well as in the Merced Grove, also in Yosemite.

Many giant sequoias are over 1,500 years old; they can attain these great ages because of their thick bark and lack of resins, which provide some protection against fire. In addition to being fire retardant, the heavy concentration of tannin in sequoias repels insects and fungi, and the tree can continue to grow even if the trunk hollows out. Sequoia groves are rather open compared to other forests, although they do grow alongside incense cedars and white firs, which they greatly overshadow.

GIANT SEQUOIA

Giant sequoia *(Sequoiadendron giganteum)*

The only way to get a true sense of the scale of the giant sequoia is to see a human being beside it. I've tried painting them numerous times, knowing that even the best artists can fall short when they try to capture the enormous majesty of these trees. The bark is a rich reddish brown and the trunk is larger at the base, buttressed much like the western redcedar. Large, fluted ridges grow up the trunk and, in the oldest specimens, the bases are bare. But younger trees have lush, blue-green foliage that reaches down almost to the ground.

The discovery of the giant sequoias in California in the 1850s resulted in some very bizarre and disrespectful (to our modern sensibilities) entertainments. One tree in the Calaveras Grove was taken down and the remaining stump planed in order to make a bowling alley. Another stump was turned into a dance floor where thirty-two people danced a cotillion.

Years ago I had to board a bus that was packed to its limit with visitors to visit the Mariposa Grove with my family. This wasn't the best way to experience Yosemite, although it's the only workable way to accommodate the huge number of travelers to the park, Yosemite Valley, and the sequoia groves. It was a hot day, and as the driver allowed the bus to fill with even more people, I found myself becoming almost panicky with claustrophobia. But once the bus released us at the grove, my anxiety subsided. I thought, how colossal, how old these trees are, how majestic. Then I wondered, would a tree ever feel fear? What could trigger that? Oncoming flames, suffocating smoke? Attributing fear to a tree seemed like pretty extreme anthropomorphism, but my human emotions were so stirred in their presence that I couldn't help but experience a lessening of the boundaries between us. Was it impossible that they might feel, too?

GIANT SEQUOIA CONE

*In some mysterious way woods
have never seemed to me to be static things.
In physical terms, I move through them;
yet in metaphysical ones,
they seem to move through me.*

—John Fowles, *The Tree*

ABOVE AND OPPOSITE: GIANT SEQUOIAS, YOSEMITE NATIONAL PARK

Champion Trees

In the 1940s the National Big Tree Program (now called the National Register of Champion Trees) was started. Of the seventy-seven trees on the first list created, a few still stand as the biggest, among them the General Sherman giant sequoia in Sequoia National Park. At over 350 feet tall, the Dyerville Giant coast redwood was once thought to be the world's tallest tree, but it was replaced by Rockefeller, at 366 feet, in 1957, which was in turn surpassed by Hyperion at 379.7 feet (the Dyerville Giant and Rockefeller are located in Humboldt Redwoods State Park, while Hyperion is located in Redwood National Park). As the program took off, more and more tree species were added.

The American Forests point system was established in the 1950s to measure trees, as arguments often arose between states about which one had the biggest or tallest trees. The point system measures diameter by using a tape measure at breast height to find the circumference, assumed to be a circle, which is divided by pi. Next the height is determined, which is a bit more complicated as a laser or clinometer is required to get really accurate measurements, by finding the angle to the top, the angle to the bottom, and the distance to the tree.

Finally crown spread is averaged. One person stands beneath the widest crown area on one side of the tree and another person pulls a tape measurer over to the opposite side. The exact same maneuver is executed under the narrowest spread of the crown, and then those two numbers are averaged.

Robert Van Pelt's book *Forest Giants of the Pacific Coast* includes some very excellent drawings of individual giants. It is almost never possible to take a photo of an individual tree, as they are surrounded by other trees in the forest, and even if one did take a photo, the curve of the camera lens (also known as parallax curve) would distort its true dimensions. So Van Pelt used his measurements to create accurate portraits of individual trees. I have not done that in my tree portraits, as verisimilitude is not really what I am after. I am trying instead to get a sense of the magnitude of a giant and its proportionate size compared to something smaller, closer to the human scale. There were deer beside these giant sequoias (page 127) when I photographed them, and that helped to establish the scale for my watercolor.

In *The Cabaret of Plants*, Richard Mabey notes that many celebrated trees were given names that alluded to politics or important political figures. Think of General Sherman at Sequoia National Park. Mabey says the "natural gravitas" of the trees somehow "annexed them to the governing elite." He goes on to remark that the champion trees attract people who may not be as interested in the survival of the species as in "prolonging the life and exact genetic essence of the veterans." About this he thinks there is a "whiff of arboreal eugenics." It's easy to overlook an entire species when one is fixated on finding the tallest and biggest specimens. For many species, continual renewal with new individuals is a much more important enterprise. Keeping all this in mind, I do have a short list of a few favorite champions:

PANDO GROVE OF ASPENS: Growing near Fish Lake, Utah, this grove is thought to be the largest organism ever, spread out over 106 acres and estimated at thirteen million pounds. It is a clone, in that it grew from one tree to make up these many apparent individuals: around forty thousand. It may be one of the oldest trees on earth, existing since the beginning of the last Ice Age, which makes it around eighty thousand years old. The name *Pando* means "I spread" in Latin.

METHUSELAH BRISTLECONE PINE: This specimen is located within Inyo National Forest in California, but its location is not available to the public, in order to protect the tree. It was 4,789 years old when it was sampled in the 1950s.

GENERAL SHERMAN GIANT SEQUOIA: The world's largest tree when measured by volume is located in Sequoia National Park and is approximately 275 feet tall. It was estimated in 1981 to contain about 52,500 cubic feet of wood.

QUINAULT BIG SITKA SPRUCE: Considered by some to be the largest Sitka spruce in the world, this tree is 191 feet high and 17.7 feet in diameter, with a crown spread of 96 feet. According to Robert Van Pelt there is some disagreement as to whether this enormous Sitka spruce, which grows on the south shore of Lake Quinault on the Olympic Peninsula, is larger than an Oregon spruce called the Klootchy Creek Giant, which had been the champion spruce since first measured in 1974. In either case, seeing either of the trees is overwhelming!

QUINAULT SITKA SPRUCE

Sugar pine *(Pinus lambertiana)*

Sugar pines can grow up to 180 feet tall with a diameter up to 42 inches. They are most common on cool western slopes from the Oregon Cascades to the Sierra Nevada. The bark of a mature tree is grayish to purplish brown, scaly, and broken up with fissures. The needles are five per bundle, 2¾ to 4 inches long. Most notable on this tree are the cones, which can be up to 24 inches long!

In California some years ago I collected a 14-inch-long sugar pine cone, much as people in the Middle Ages once collected what they thought were the wonders of nature. Narwhal tusks, for instance, were much sought after as people believed them to be unicorn horns, and thus imbued with magical properties and healing powers. Narwhal tusks were hung from the ceilings of cathedrals, tangible objects that symbolized Christ.

I decided to hang my pine cone in the carport of my house. (You can often find sugar pine cones at Christmas tree lots, next to the wreaths.) The one I sketched here, although not the largest one I had ever seen, was worth celebrating with a watercolor. I placed it beside a coffee cup so the scale of the cone could be better appreciated.

Pacific dogwood *(Cornus nuttallii)*

The Pacific dogwood is found from southern British Columbia all the way to the San Bernardino Mountains in California; in hotter conditions they thrive at higher elevations. What appear to be enormous white flowers, up to six inches across, are actually bracts—small, leaflike structures positioned between the flowers. The true flowers are tiny clusters, in the center between the bracts, that ripen into red fruit in the fall. Another example of this type of flower is the Christmas poinsettia.

I have painted dogwoods in two seasons and in various places. While in damper forests the tree achieves greater heights—up to fifty feet, in the Pacific Northwest—the fall colors can be less noticeable as autumn storms tend to rip the leaves from the trees or make them so sodden that they turn brown. Though dogwoods grow at Yosemite, I would have perhaps not have noticed them except that the fall color made the shrubs stand out from the rest of the understory plants. Some of the most spectacular dogwoods I have seen are in the sequoia groves at Yosemite.

**PACIFIC DOGWOOD,
YOSEMITE NATIONAL PARK**

ABOVE: PACIFIC DOGWOOD BRACTS, OPPOSITE: PACIFIC DOGWOODS IN AUTUMN

Subalpine Forests

southern

Jeffrey pine
whitebark pine
limber pine
lodgepole pine
western white pine
mountain hemlock
Sierra lodgepole pine
mountain sorrel
fireweed
alpine chipmunk
mountain beaver
hermit thrush
Swainson's thrush

northern

common juniper
western mountain ash
redosier dogwood
Cascade azalea
Scouler's willow
red mountain heather
explorer's gentian
avalanche lily
mountain goat
marmot
ptarmigan
Canada jay
hairy woodpecker
calliope hummingbird
red-breasted sapsucker

Few people gazing out upon a timberline for the first time can imagine how many interacting phenomena are involved in this "forest frontier."

—Stephen F. Arno, from the preface to *Timberline*

Some of the happiest hiking I have done in my life has taken place in subalpine forests, and these places have inspired my best art. Subalpine refers to the area between timberline, which no trees grow above, and the middle elevations of the montane zone. The subalpine forests of the West are southern extensions of the boreal forest, which covers Alaska, Canada, and other similar latitudes across the globe. During the last Ice Age the boreal conifers retreated south to the mountain zones. When glaciers covered the higher elevations, the conifers moved down the mountains to lower slopes and across basins and valleys. But then warming forced the trees back into the mountains and they became isolated, as sagebrush and grasses took over the lower elevations.

According to Stephen Whitney, author of the *National Audubon Society Nature Guide: Western Forests*, the subalpine zone has different features depending on elevation. At the lowest elevations are closed forests, much like the forests found farther down the mountains. Next are areas where difficult climate and growing conditions limit the number of trees that can grow. Finally, at the upper limit, is the parkland or woodland portion, made up of small groves or tree islands. (See "Timberline Survivors" later in this chapter.)

In the north, in Washington and Oregon, subalpine forests consist primarily of mountain hemlock and subalpine fir. Farther east, in the Rockies, subalpine fir and Engelmann spruce are the primary species. In the Sierra Nevada, mountain hemlock is still dominant, but there are also whitebark pine, lodgepole pine, and foxtail pine. In the Great Basin area, bristlecone and limber pine live at timberline.

Northern Subalpine Forests

The combination of forest and meadow in the northern subalpine ecoregions is simply unparalleled in beauty. Plentiful precipitation, falling as rain and snow in the Pacific Northwest, creates lush alpine meadows and dense forests of subalpine firs at the higher elevations. I've done countless paintings and sketches of these places as I've been hiking there my whole life. Places like Mount Rainier are ideal because you can drive up to the elevations where these trees and plants thrive. In so many other areas, the prelude is a long, difficult hike up several thousand feet.

Alaska cedar *(Callitropsis nootkatensis)*

Alaska cedars are among my favorite species because of their hardiness in the alpine environment. The trees are found in coastal mountains from south central Alaska to southwestern Oregon, and grow best between 2,500 and 6,500 feet of elevation. They are happiest in a maritime climate where rain and snow are plentiful; they also require moderate temperatures that rarely fall below 0 degrees Fahrenheit. You can see them growing in very rocky soils—if there is enough fog and rain they thrive even where the soil layer is quite thin. These cedars can grow as krummholz (contorted and small) trees, extending across rocky ridges at high altitude, their beautiful draping branches like arms loaded with blue-gray needles.

Alaska cedars require more light than other alpine species, and so can be crowded out by the subalpine firs. They can also reach venerable ages; it is thought they can live for as long as two thousand years. Mature cedars slightly below the subalpine can be up to 130 feet tall. One of the biggest trees in Mount Rainier National Park grows in the Ipsut Creek valley just northeast of Ipsut Pass. The trees here are over twelve hundred years old.

The bark of the Alaska cedar is grayish white in mature trees, but in younger trees it is scaly, with a pink color, streaked with darker areas. The needles come in flat sprays and die off after two years, turning yellow or brown, which can give the trees a slightly unhealthy look, although I haven't seen this often at Mount Rainier National Park. The seed cones are about ½ inch in diameter and are dispersed by the wind.

There is a remarkable ten-acre relict group of cedars growing in a cool, north-facing ravine in the Aldrich Mountains of central Oregon. This is about 140 miles east of the tree's normal habitat in the Cascades. Biohistorians think that Alaska cedars may have grown all over the Pacific Northwest during the last Ice Age, when conditions were much cooler and wetter east of the Cascades.

ALASKA CEDARS AT SUNRISE, MOUNT RAINIER NATIONAL PARK

MOUNT RAINIER AND SUBALPINE FIRS NEAR NISQUALLY VISTA

Trees of the West

Subalpine fir *(Abies lasiocarpa)*

Subalpine firs are perhaps one of the most iconic species of the western mountains. Once past the sapling stage their narrow growth and spired crowns make them unmistakable. This tree is the most widespread fir in the west, ranging from the Yukon Territory through the Rockies to New Mexico and Arizona. But it is limited to the higher elevations. On the west slope of the Cascades it grows from 4,000 to 7,000 feet, but in the Rockies it requires the cooler temperatures that prevail from 9,000 to 12,000 feet. It prefers moist soils but can survive in drier conditions as well.

The two watercolors on the following pages show subalpine firs growing on both the west side and the east side of Mount Rainier. Notice the very thin shape of the firs near Berkeley Park. Even though it is sometimes called an alpine fir, the tree really is subalpine. Alpine plant species thrive in tundralike conditions, above the tree line, where freezing temperatures and radiation are so extreme that trees cannot survive; the subalpine fir only reaches the limit of tree line.

Subalpine firs can grow as high as sixty to one hundred feet, but they are not especially long lived, achieving a maximum lifespan of perhaps 250 years. The bark of the tree is gray with small, resinous blisters, and it becomes more fissured as it ages. Like other true firs, the dark purple cones appear upright atop upper branches.

These trees will often layer in climates with severe conditions, which means they put down heavy skirts of branches toward the bottom of the trunk, and those branches then root themselves. After many such rootings, there may be an entire colony of firs. These tree colonies, or islands, are common at Mount Rainier National Park and are an essential element of the dramatic scenery there.

In Their Time

I like to be there—
late spring at the far reaches of treeline—
when the mountain hemlock and subalpine fir
first break out of the deep snowpack:
soft-sliding blanket that had laid them
bough and stem to the slope
while the weight of winter moved past.

It's the warmth of the life in these small trees
slowly melts through the frozen grip,
and on a day of sun-loosened crust,
a break-through-to-your-knees day full of juncos
and the skittery tracks of marmot,
they will upturn like a drawn bow
and with a sudden springing burst of snow
right themselves once more into treehood.

I like to think of the one winter
when each of them, thickened with the years
of snowmelt and wind,
find that singular strength to hold straight
through the deepening snows;
to have turned the great bows of their trunks
into the slope, and held there;
lifting, finally
out of the slow dance of the years
as all things lift in their time.

—Tim McNulty, from *In Blue Mountain Dusk*

A MEADOW AT PARADISE IN MOUNT RAINIER NATIONAL PARK

SUBALPINE FIRS ABOVE BERKELEY PARK AT MOUNT RAINIER NATIONAL PARK

Whitebark pine *(Pinus albicaulis)*

I never noticed the whitebark pines until my first visit to Crater Lake. Bleached snags jut out over the crater rim and shine against the cobalt blue of the lake and the expanse of the sky (page 144). You only realize that the trees are still living when you see the new growth near the ground in areas of snowmelt. After I saw them there, I began to look for them everywhere. They rise from near death in so many places. At 6,000 feet in elevation along the Wonderland Trail above Sunrise at Mount Rainier. In the black lava lands of central Oregon. At Blue Lake beneath the Early Winters Spires in the North Cascades. At Tioga Pass, the eastern entry point of Yosemite.

The trees range from Washington south to central California and east to western Wyoming, growing at 4,500 to 7,000 feet in the north and 8,000 to 12,000 feet in the south. These higher elevations expose trees to heavy snow burdens, drying winds, ultraviolet light, and summer drought. In drier sites, the pines are also at a higher risk for beetle infestation. With many subalpine species, like mountain hemlocks and subalpine firs, the signs of struggle are not obvious. For those trees, even in high-altitude situations, foliage is often lush, and trees sometimes grow tall. In optimal conditions, the whitebark pine can reach fifty feet in height, its needles in bundles of five and the cones 1½ to 3¼ inches long, purple to brown. But near tree line, the whitebark pine becomes little more than a shrub, and it hides nothing of the severity of its life.

I saw this whitebark pine at Cutthroat Pass in the North Cascades. Here there is ample moisture, the tree still catching much of the precipitation of Pacific storms, and so it is growing rather lushly compared to many of the other specimens I've represented in my art.

I love the song of tree and wind
How beautiful they sing

—**John Clare,** from the poem "The Wind and Trees"

Mountain hemlock *(Tsuga mertensiana)*

Mountain hemlocks thrive in the subalpine and alpine tundra zones, where the climate consists of short, cool summers with wet autumns and heavy winter snow cover that lasts for five to nine months. Elevations range from 1,000 to 7,500 feet depending on geographic location; the elevation limits decrease from south to north and from east to west. Mountain hemlocks can reach more than eight hundred years of age and often mix with subalpine fir, Alaska cedar, Pacific silver fir, whitebark pine, Engelmann spruce, and subalpine larch. They can grow even on volcanic soils as long as the moisture is adequate. Mountain hemlocks are easy to identify because of their delicate foliage and the way in which their needles emerge from the branches in a star or asterisk pattern. They take on many forms at exposed high altitudes, which is one of their most beautiful attributes. At lower elevations in the subalpine parkland zone, they can achieve great heights and are among the most common species.

The Park Butte Trail in the North Cascades begins in lush Schriebers Meadow and steeply climbs to the Railroad Grade Trail, on a lateral moraine of the Easton Glacier of Mount Baker. East of the Park Butte fire lookout are glorious high alpine parklands with tree islands, tarns, flowery meadows in summer, and Mount Baker taking up the entire view to the north. It was there that my friend and I encountered a miraculous grove of mountain hemlocks, a single organism with multiple trunks—I have been creating paintings and prints based on that experience ever since. My first effort was a watercolor focused on color (page 146): I wanted to reveal the sparkling contrast of the emerald meadows, the dark hemlock foliage, and the pristine white of Mount Baker. I tried a block print version of the hemlock as well (page 147), where form and value take precedence over color, as black-and-white contrast is the essence of the relief print. I only add color to the prints after the oil-based ink has been rolled on the block, printed, and finally allowed to dry. (See the section on printmaking in the Introduction.)

Mountain Hemlock

"Look at the stars," you said,
"the whole tree is covered with stars."

And it was true—
tiny whorls of needles
glistening in reflected light.

Ever since that time,
I don't remember where or when,
I always look for the stars,
and seeing them, see your laughing face.

So today, high in a cirque basin
at timberline, with granite and
waterfalls all around,

I see one small orange and black butterfly
a fritillary, fanning its wings
on a stunted mountain hemlock.

The whole night sky reflected there,
And where are you?

—Saul Weisberg, from *Headwaters*

OPPOSITE AND ABOVE: MOUNTAIN HEMLOCK AND MOUNT BAKER, WASHINGTON

Portions of the Pacific Crest Trail can be easily approached from major highways; we found a section of the trail just south of Stevens Pass off Highway 2. Our hike began as we passed under ski lifts—not the most aesthetic of sights—but we quickly left them behind. Soon we reached a ridgetop where flowers were still blooming in September and a mass of Mormon fritillary butterflies were sipping nectar from pearly everlasting and fireweed. Farther along the trail to the south, very close to Lake Susan Jane in the Alpine Lakes Wilderness Area, I saw this magnificent old hemlock (opposite) leaning out precariously over the steeply canted mountainside. The provisional and tenuous aspects of existence are never far from one's mind in the high country, and to find a very old survivor like this was a most uplifting sight!

Subalpine larch *(Larix lyallii)*

The subalpine larch grows at timberline and is often the pioneer species at the nose of glaciers or at the base of avalanche chutes. The tree is found from 6,000 to 9,000 feet in elevation and grows in a very limited number of locations, including the North Cascades and Glacier National Parks, and the Bob Marshall, Glacier Peak, and Pasayten Wilderness Areas. It is also a much-appreciated and often photographed inhabitant of the Alpine Lakes Wilderness Area. It grows with Engelmann spruce, subalpine fir, and whitebark pine.

Subalpine larches have been known to grow as tall as ninety feet, although I have never seen such a large specimen. The height of an old tree can be over fifty feet with a trunk diameter of two feet. The needles are a delicate pale green, very short at 1 to 1¼ inches, growing very densely on the twigs. They appear in bunches of thirty to forty, and in spring the lovely blue-green color subtly sets them apart from other conifers. The seed cones are purple and grow upright on the branches.

The subalpine larch is a remarkable tree. In summer you're most likely scarcely aware of it as a separate species, since it has needles like its associates, the subalpine fir and the Engelmann spruce. But it is the rare deciduous conifer—leafless at high elevations for eight months out of the year—and in autumn its brilliant color is unmistakable, a gold somewhere between deep yellow and bronze. I have been moved to make art about these trees many times, in block prints where I can capture the intense contrast between the golds of the trees and the deep greens of the evergreen conifers, or in watercolors where the deep yellows subtly blend with the creams, browns, and golds of the Golden Horn Batholith, found just of Highway 20 in the North Cascades.

But for me it isn't just the fall colors. I was hiking one overcast August day at Cutthroat Pass in the North Cascades as light rain fell, a far from perfect day, and yet I was so moved by the beauty of the young larches and their graceful blue-green new growth; they were far more interesting than any of the expansive views I experienced that day. I marveled at their short growing season: how late it was, early August, and they had just donned their new needles! Needles soon to fall, in October—a brief but glorious season of beauty.

EARLY WINTER SPIRES AND LARCHES IN THE NORTH CASCADES

YOUNG LARCHES, WASHINGTON PASS

HALF DOME FROM OLMSTEAD POINT

Southern Subalpine Forests

The Sierra Nevada and Great Basin subalpine forests are complex and feature different species depending on the latitude and amount of rainfall. North of Lake Tahoe, the forests include mountain hemlock, and California red fir. Farther south in the central and southern Sierra Nevada there are large areas near timberline covered in granite where trees have a much harder time gaining a foothold. In these more southerly forests you will find Sierra lodgepole pine, whitebark pine, limber pine, Jeffrey pine, Sierra juniper, and foxtail pine, the latter perhaps the most picturesque of the conifer family in the Sierra Nevada. Great Basin bristlecone pine is also a subalpine species of the south, but only in the scattered Great Basin mountain ranges of the Mojave Desert, including the White Mountains.

Three species stand out for me in the Sierra Nevada subalpine zone. The first is the red fir, prominent in the moister areas in the range, a tree whose beauty extends throughout its lifespan, from small saplings to trees as old as half a millennium. The other two trees are the Sierra juniper and the foxtail pine.

My husband and I first saw the red firs along the trail to The Fissures in Yosemite early one October morning. We walked past smaller trees in the shade, lit up by sun pouring through gaps in the canopy created by the mature trees. The young trees' blue-green needles were radiant where the light struck them, and I had to make a watercolor of it (page 162).

Driving up to Tuolumne afterward, we saw immense stands of red fir with no other trees. I remember wanting to jump out of the car so I could walk through and discover what it felt like to be in those groves. How would the air smell, what would the ambient light be? Time didn't allow on that trip, but I am determined to go back and take that walk.

Just a little closer to Tuolumne we saw the ancient junipers of Olmsted Point, and I had to go scramble around on the granite. Farther east toward Tioga Pass we saw stands of juniper looking exactly like a grocer's display of broccoli set on end, almost comical, yet the trees were so old that they commanded my respect.

An Ancient Bristlecone Pine Forest

White Mountains, California

Here on their mountaintop
it's all rock, sun, and stubby trees,
the trunks twisted
inside out, more
bare grain than bark,
as if the oldest trees on Earth
were writhing to leave it.
The ripping storms
of four thousand winters
have cropped their limbs
to broken brushes
of blunt needles.
Yet somehow
what they need
is here, surrounded
in sky, where scree
drifts downslope
faster than trees can grow.
Open brown cones
gather around the trunks—
the steady reply
to wind, snow, and centuries
from roots clenched in stone.

—John Daniel, from
Of Earth: New and Selected Poems

Great Basin bristlecone pine *(Pinus longaeva)*

The Great Basin bristlecone pine grows between 10,000 and 11,500 feet of elevation in the White Mountains of eastern California. Methuselah, the grandaddy of them all at 4,854 years old (as of April 2022), is the most ancient non-clonal tree on earth.

In spite of the bitter cold and drought that the bristlecone must endure, it can grow a rather straight trunk, though many are quite contorted. Some of the trees are as tall as sixty feet with five-foot diameters. The needles are deep green in groups of five. Cones are 2½ to 3½ inches long, and dark purplish brown. Unlike most other pines, the bristlecone needles are not shed after a few years—they can persist for up to forty years. Growth ring analyses on the pines have shown that some of them have up to four thousand rings, which is proof of the four thousand years they have lived.

Bristlecones seem to live the longest at the highest elevations, which is rather contrary to what one would expect. Conditions are much less severe lower down, but there they are susceptible to lower elevation fungi and insects and even porcupines feeding on their bark. The bristlecones that live at low elevation sites grow faster and die younger.

Foxtail pine *(Pinus balfouriana)*

I don't think I can describe this tree any better than the Dutch botanist Aljos Farjon did in *A Natural History of Cedars*: "On a long ridge below Mineral Peak, at 10,150 feet in the southern Sierra Nevada of California, there is a pine wood. It is the most beautiful stand of conifers I have ever seen. The impressive, bright orange trunks are ornamented with squamate patterns like the back of an alligator, above them sturdy branches are clothed in deep green foliage looking like thousands of squirrel tails, all set against the bluest of blue skies."

Farjon goes on to say that these conifers have adapted to very harsh growing conditions—no soil, months of winter snow and cold, high altitudes, summers of drought. I marvel that such a beautiful tree could be the result of such a difficult and punishing environment.

The foxtail pine consists of two subspecies: the southern *balfouriana*, which grows near Sequoia and Kings Canyon National Parks in the Sierra Nevada, and the northern *austrina*, which grows in the Klamath Mountains. There is some speculation about how long the two subspecies have been separated—anywhere from hundreds of thousands to millions of years. But they are closely related.

Like the bristlecones, the foxtails are five-needled soft pines with cone scales that are thick on the surface with a prickle or spine. The needles are short and densely packed some distance down the twig. They do not branch as much as the other pines, which is how they got the name "foxtail." (John Muir called them "bottle-brush tassels.")

The northern foxtails tend to grow straighter and are more fully crowned with needles and branches. They grow from 6,000 to 8,000 feet in elevation, often on south-facing slopes. The southern foxtails are usually found alongside granite boulders from 9,000 to 11,300 feet in elevation. They are widely spaced, almost as if planted in an alpine garden. There is some speculation that the southern species may live up to three thousand years of age, but there is no documentation of that. Their growth habit is much more picturesque than the northern subspecies. The leader branches die back, leaving twisted, needle-free treetops; the trunks twist as the bark sloughs off, with small remaining strips of bark diagonally traversing the bare wood of the trunks. The effect is like the most beautiful bonsai specimen you could imagine, only much larger.

From my journal:

All year I have been planning to go down to Kings Canyon to see the foxtail pines. The Sierra foxtail pine has been my version of Matthiessen's Himalayan snow leopard. I knew it would take a long bumpy drive on a forest service gravel road, or else an arduous hike of over ten miles. I was ready and willing to do that, figuring I would fly to Fresno and rent a car . . . But then the pandemic struck, and all my plans, along with everyone else's, went nowhere.

Aljos Farjon's words about these foxtails being the most beautiful stand of conifers he had ever seen haunted me. He has been everywhere, all over the world, seeking out conifers, as head of the Herbarium at the Royal Botanic Gardens at Kew. And I had seen photos that beckoned

BRISTLECONE PINE (I USED A PEN TO ACCENTUATE THE TRUNK FISSURE IN THIS WATERCOLOR.)

FOXTAIL PINE

me—the foxtails' beautiful bark standing out against the blue of a sky seen at high altitude, their rich-hued sienna trunks growing at careless angles to snow in winter, or granite in summer. How strange to think that a tree is as elusive as the snow leopard. This tree, more than any other I have learned about, has succeeded in the "strategy of evasion" that Farjon describes as the way of life of conifers—evading not only the broadleaved trees and other conifers, but also me. Perhaps I like the foxtail even more now, its remoteness keeping me from knowing it, painting or photographing it. It has its own life, separate from me.

Sierra juniper *(Juniperus grandis)*

Until 2006, when genetic testing elevated it to its own species, the Sierra juniper was mistakenly assumed to be a subspecies of the western juniper. It favors shallow, rocky soils in mountains, in drier areas and higher elevations. The juniper's height is usually from ten to thirty feet (and can sometimes reach 100 feet), but very old giants, up to two thousand years old with diameters as large as sixteen feet, can be found on rocky outcrops. Young trees have pinkish bark, but as they age the bark becomes reddish and shredded and often deeply furrowed. Leaves are scalelike, 1⁄16 inch long, and dark gray green. The blueish-black berries are elliptical, not round.

The Sierra juniper I painted (pages 158–159) grows near Olmsted Point in Yosemite National Park. It's found along Highway 120, also known as the Tioga Road, as it heads east to Tuolumne Meadows. The sight of this thousand-year-old tree grasping for sustenance in the bare granite was utterly thrilling. I don't really enjoy being in photos, but here I asked my husband to photograph me as I posed near the tree, which I couldn't seem to tear myself away from. I honestly did not want to leave.

TECHNIQUE
Cast Shadows

Sometimes the foreground of a painting can be somewhat uninteresting. One very useful technique for breaking up the foreground is to paint cast shadows. I usually use a blue, either cobalt or ultramarine, and sometimes I mix a little bit of violet into it as well, as in this detail of the juniper's cast shadows. In addition to interrupting a flat area of color, this technique can also help make a landscape look more accurate and three-dimensional. Here the viewer can see that the light is very steeply angled and might even guess that it is autumn.

Timberline Survivors

In his book *Timberline: Mountain and Arctic Forest Frontiers*, Stephen Arno writes about the various conditions that trees at timberline have to contend with. Among them are extreme cold, poor substrates (underling rock or soil), intense solar radiation, high winds, and heavy snow through much of the year, alternating with summer drought. All of these factors can interact in interesting ways, creating patterns of growth that make hiking timberline trails especially interesting. Arno describes a phenomenon called "ridgetop ribbon forest," which occurs in certain sites in western Montana. Small windrows of trees grow atop broad ridges, yet are surrounded on the windward side by more drought-typical bunchgrass and Idaho fescue. On the lee, snow glades are filled with sedges, while downslope a mature, deep subalpine forest thrives.

Most fascinating perhaps are the growth forms that individual trees develop to cope with the extreme conditions. Of course, some trees manage to grow very straight and tall—in the Colorado Rockies there are some Engelmann spruce groves with enormous trees. Subalpine fir can also achieve great heights; a visitor to Mount Rainier National Park will find many alpine meadow forests with tall firs. But the stunted and contorted trees seem to garner the most attention. Trees that are exposed to high winds often develop branches only on the lee side, sometimes resulting in flagged krummholz; in these trees, there is a small banner of foliage at the top of the tree, where most of the needles and branches have been sheared off or otherwise destroyed by the weather. Another form is cushion krummholz, where trees attain only a few inches of height, spreading out horizontally instead, sometimes as much as fifty feet. Other trees develop large tree skirts with lower branches, protected by snow from the worst effects of the wind and dryness.

It is quite common to find tree islands in more barren environments. Growing in clusters, huddling together as it were, protects some of the trees from the wind and temperature extremes. It also provides what Arno calls the "black-body effect," wherein their darkness causes snow to melt faster, thus warming them more quickly as winter ends and providing slightly more optimal conditions for their spring growth.

I was completely captivated by the multiple trunks of this tree island. The grove may have begun with one tall individual bent into the earth by wind and heavy snow that then produced offspring through layering—the lower branches, pressed into the moist ground, developed roots, which then sent up erect stems. The multitrunk growth habit is very advantageous in this ecological niche, transforming the individual tree into a colonylike organism that protects each trunk of it. Alaska cedars, some firs, spruce, and, as in the etching here, mountain hemlocks, are able to layer on moist and snowy sites. Prostrate branches of the "mother" tree take root; new trees may appear separate but have, in fact, the identical genetic makeup to the original tree. This type of regeneration is most common at timberline.

To create the etching, I drew all of the line work onto a copper plate, etched that first (by dropping the plate into an acid bath), and then considered the tones or values that I wanted to achieve. Everything without tone is masked before applying the aquatint rosin, and the plate is immersed in the acid in successive stages. So only the sky was protected from darker tones in the first acid bath, where the lightest values were added. Then I began masking additional areas in order to create different tones. By the last acid bath, only the darkest trunks and foliage were still exposed.

I saw this hemlock grove near the Railroad Grade Trail at the base of Mount Baker. It was difficult to say which was more remarkable—the view of Mount Baker or the tree islands in the high meadow.

California red fir *(Abies magnifica)*

The California red fir can grow to 230 feet, with a diameter of ten feet, and live as long as five hundred years. Although the tree can be found in the upper elevations of the Sierra Nevada (from 4,600 to 9,000 feet) with pines and mountain hemlock, it is most magnificent when you encounter a pure stand at the higher elevations. The trees prefer open, sunny areas where snowfall accumulates—in a wet year, up to thirty feet. Donald Culross Peattie described their preferred habitat as a "snow forest."

Saplings have a cool blue-green hue and perfect Christmas tree shape, but as the trees age, they become less regular and with more gaps in the branching along the trunk. At that point the trunks take on a rich reddish-purple, almost maroon, color.

Red firs earned the name "silvertip fir" because of the beautiful color of the young needles, which are short and blunt. The cones can be up to nine inches in length and are purplish brown. A related species, the Shasta fir, which grows near Sequoia and Kings Canyon National Parks, and then from Lassen Peak to Crater Lake, has cones with bracts, unlike the red fir.

In the high elevation reaches of the western portion of Yosemite National Park red firs grow in great numbers. We saw them one morning in late October near Glacier Point, where Teddy Roosevelt and John Muir famously met more than a century ago, along the Taft Point and Fissures Trail.

From my journal:

> It was so early in the morning that there was no one on the trail. The sun shone on bracken ferns turning golden at the foot of the enormous firs. As they age, the firs' bark thickens and turns a beautiful deep red, with hints of violet. The forest was cool, dampened by a recent rain, sun-dappled and so impossibly quiet that we startled a deer in the shade of the deeper forest.
>
> The young firs were illuminated by the morning light—how different they were from the mature trees—their blue-green needles perhaps the freshest, most beautiful color I have seen in nature.
>
> We came back out into the open near Taft Point and crossed close to The Fissures, where two masses of rock had fractured naturally along the joint lines. It is thought these massive granite faces are like many others in Yosemite, the only difference being that these have not slipped so far apart. The view through the foot-wide cranny thousands of feet below to the valley floor was startling, dizzying.
>
> At the end of the trail we looked down on El Capitan—from that vantage point its 3,600 feet of sheer wall seemed almost inconsequential. And the busy Valley became miniaturized. What a perspective of the grand sights of Yosemite, on a trail that had just revealed its own glory, in the form of the red firs.

CALIFORNIA RED FIR, YOSEMITE NATIONAL PARK

Deserts

Great Basin

singleleaf pinyon pine
Great Basin bristlecone pine
Rocky Mountain juniper
big sagebrush
gray rabbitbrush
prickly pear cactus
greenleaf manzanita
greasewood
fourwing saltbush
arrowleaf balsamroot
mule deer
yellow-bellied marmot
bighorn sheep
mountain lion
bobcat
western meadowlark
red-naped sapsucker
red-tailed hawk

Mojave

singleleaf pinyon pine
California juniper
shrub live oak
desert willow
creosote bush
bighorn sheep
mountain lion
jackrabbit
gila monster
roadrunner
burrowing owl
Scott's oriole
hairy scorpion

Sonoran

brittlebush
desert marigold
fishhook barrel cactus
kangaroo rat
javelina
roadrunner
gila woodpecker
screech-owl
Gambel's quail
cactus wren
desert tortoise
tarantula

Chihuahuan

prickly pear cactus
desert spoon
century plant
creosote bush
mule deer
pronghorn
kit fox
jaguar
prairie dog
earless lizard
elf owl
band-tailed pigeon
vermilion flycatcher
pygmy nuthatch

The United States has four major deserts: the Great Basin, Mojave, Sonoran, and Chihuahuan. Three of the deserts are classified as "hot"—the Mojave, Sonoran, and Chihuahuan—because of their high temperatures and long summers. The plant life in those deserts is more closely related to the subtropical plant communities to the south than to the mountains that surround them. Some biologists and geologists think the Mojave is not really a desert with its own characteristics, but rather a transition zone between the Great Basin and Sonoran Deserts.

The Four Corners, which includes Arches and Grand Canyon National Parks, as well as the southwestern corner of Colorado, the southeastern corner of Utah, the northeastern corner of Arizona, and the northwestern corner of New Mexico, is not considered by some to be a desert at all. Or, there are those who think of it as an extension of the Great Basin Desert, while still others designate the Four Corners as a separate desert entirely: the Painted Desert. As with so many designations and classifications, these arbitrary geographical boundaries were created by humans to simplify the natural world—plants, animals, and birds don't stop moving when they reach state lines—and they may thrive in what appears to us to be inhospitable conditions. The art for this section includes several prints that feature birds whose presence enlivens the arid landscapes.

CACTUS WREN

ARROWLEAF BALSAMROOT IN BLOOM IN GREAT BASIN DESERT

Great Basin Desert

The Great Basin Desert is found in eastern Oregon, southern Idaho, Nevada, eastern Utah, and northern-most Arizona. Its parameters are based on how water flows—called the Hydrographic Great Basin—with the precipitation here evaporating, sinking underground, or flowing into primarily saline lakes. There is no flow to the Pacific Ocean or the Gulf of Mexico. The climate is partially the result of it being in the rain shadow of the Cascade Range in the north and the Sierra Nevada in the south. It is the most sparsely populated area of the United States. The two largest cities in the Great Basin Desert are Salt Lake City, Utah, on its eastern edge, and Reno, Nevada, on its western edge. It is the farthest north of the deserts, and because of the freezing winter temperatures it has the most limited plant life. Vegetation is primarily low, small-leafed shrubs like big sagebrush and greasewood.

Utah juniper *(Juniperus osteosperma)*

A smaller variety, the Utah juniper grows from fifteen to fifty feet in height, with yellow-green, scalelike leaves. Its cones develop as berries, mealy in texture and not quite as sweet as those of the Rocky Mountain juniper. It also grows with pinyons and is quite common in the Grand Canyon and other Southwest can-yonlands. As it ages it becomes beautifully twisted and contorted.

MOUNTAIN BLUEBIRD AND JUNIPER

TECHNIQUE
Etching trunk lines with an aquarelle brush

A special tool can come in handy when trying to depict the beautiful, deeply etched lines in the trunk of an ancient juniper. It could be as simple as a credit card, or anything sharp enough to press into the watercolor paper without ripping or damaging it. In this case I used the end of a watercolor brush, a specific type called an aquarelle (French for watercolor) brush, which has an angled handle that forms a sharp edge. I created other lines by applying them with saturated paint on a brush. I used white Posca pens and white gouache to show the raised and highlighted areas of the trunk.

Mojave Desert

The Mojave Desert is in Southern California, extreme southern Nevada, and the lower elevations of northwestern Arizona. Las Vegas is the major city of the Mojave. Unlike the other deserts it has a winter rainy season, when it can freeze, but not so often or as severely as in the Great Basin Desert. The Joshua tree is one of the few treelike plants here, forming "forests" above 3,000 feet. Plant life consists largely of low shrubs.

Down on my hearth-rug of desert, sage of the mesa,
An ash-grey pelt
Of wolf all hairy and level, a wolf's wild pelt.

—D. H. Lawrence, from *Autumn at Taos*

Joshua tree *(Yucca brevifolia)*

The Joshua tree, as a member of the agave family, is not technically a tree. Its namesake national park is located in California, situated between the Mojave and Colorado desert ecosystems. It is also found in the Sonoran Desert in Arizona and grows alongside pines in the San Bernardino Mountains of Southern California. Mormon settlers named it after the Old Testament hero who defeated his enemies—its arms perhaps like the arms of a warrior, or possibly reaching out in prayer.

Some Joshua trees can grow up to forty feet high, but most are not that large. They grow very slowly, ½ to 3 inches per year, and their average lifespan is 150 years, although there was one individual in the Antelope Valley thought to be over one thousand years old, which was described in a 1932 article in the *Journal of the New York Botanical Garden*. It was eighty feet high with a circumference of nine feet. On a recent road trip between Las Vegas and Palm Desert, I realized that each of the hundreds of Joshua trees I was seeing were unique individuals—not a single one looked like its brethern! The Joshua tree blooms every few years, and it is pollinated solely by the yucca moth; the moth is dependent on the seeds of the trees to nourish its larvae. Scott's orioles place their nests in the Joshua tree and sip nectar from its flowering stalks.

JOSHUA TREES

Pointleaf manzanita

(Arctostaphylos pungens)

Pointleaf manzanita is a member of the heather family, which becomes obvious when you see the whitish-pink, urn-shaped flowers so familiar to alpine meadow hikers. Manzanita is a larger shrub than heather, but it also grows in thickets, preferring hillsides. Birds eat the berries that form from the flowers. Like the madrone tree, also a member of the heather or Ericaceae family, the manzanita has a dramatic reddish bark.

Manzanita

woolly-twigged
tree with garnet bark
beneath your limbs hide
ten kinds of scorpion   at least one hairy
Sphinx moth   tarantula   burrowing owl
long-eared jackrabbit taking his moment's rest
pointleaf manzanita   you're the
Mojave senorita

—Jane Graham George

MANZANITA

CACTUS WREN WITH ORGAN PIPE CACTI IN THE BACKGROUND

Sonoran Desert

The Sonoran Desert ranges from southeast California to Baja California and Arizona. It is the most recognizably desertlike of the four major deserts, and is home to saguaro and organ pipe cactus. It encompasses many major urban areas, including Phoenix, Tucson, and Palm Springs. From December to March, the Pacific Ocean brings rain to the desert. From July to mid-September there are summer monsoons, with brief periods of wet tropical rain and frequent thunderstorms. Predators in the Sonoran Desert include owls, coyotes, bobcats, and badgers, which eat insects, lizards, frogs, and rodents.

Organ pipe cactus *(Stenocereus thurberi)*

A giant of the Sonoran Desert, the organ pipe cactus puts forth several narrow stems, which rise vertically and can reach up to twenty-six feet tall. The lavender-white flowers, which are pollinated by bats, are 2½ inches long and bloom at night. The organ pipe can live over 150 years but begins to flower only after it's about 35 years old. This cactus produces a fruit with edible red flesh flavored a bit like watermelon, but it is about the size of a tennis ball. Organ Pipe Cactus National Monument in Arizona is an ideal place to see the cactus. Cactus are a favorite roost of the aptly named cactus wren (above); unlike other wrens, these bold inhabitants of the desert often appear in the open. They don't lift up their tails as other wrens do; they fan out their tail feathers, as if to display the white tips.

SAGUARO CACTUS

Saguaro cactus *(Carnegiea gigantea)*

The saguaro is found exclusively in the Sonoran Desert in southern Arizona. Some individuals grow up to twenty-five arms, shaped like a candelabra, and reach a height of sixty-six feet. It can live up to two hundred years and is the largest cactus in the United States. The cactus is covered with protective spines and has dramatic white flowers in the late spring and reddish-purple fruit in summer. The fruit is used to make jellies, candies, and ceremonial wine by the people of the Tohono O'odham Nation, while the saguaro seeds are used as chicken feed. Gila woodpeckers and gilded flickers peck holes in the stems of the cactus, inside of which they build their nests. Once the woodpeckers abandon the cavities, elf owls, screech-owls, purple martins, and finches can move in.

It is unusual to come upon such an enormous plant in the desert. It takes a lot of water and nutrition to achieve a large size, but the saguaro has strategies for survival that allow it to grow. Unfortunately, in the spring of 2021, the cactus displayed a bizarre bloom behavior, setting flowers along the spine lower down rather than their usual placement atop the arms. Botanists think it may be the result of the extreme drought conditions that prevailed for the previous several years, stunting the arm growth. Since it takes nearly one hundred years for this cactus to reach full maturity, there is hope that there will be greater rain in future years and that the bloom habit will return to normal.

Chihuahuan Desert

The Chihuahuan Desert is the southernmost of the United States deserts, ranging from New Mexico to Texas, at a relatively high altitude—from 3,000 to 5,000 feet in elevation. It also extends into northern Mexico. In Texas it is referred to as the Trans-Pecos area, which includes the city of El Paso. In New Mexico, both Albuquerque and Las Cruces lie within the Chihuahuan. Winter can be cold, and there are winter freezes, but even so, this desert supports more than 130 species of mammals, including mule deer, prong-horn, kit fox, prairie dogs, and jackrabbits. Bird species include roadrunners and many raptors. Trees are rare, so vegetation consists of low shrubs, leaf succulents, and small cactus. Beargrass, yuccas, agave, and desert spoon are common plants, as well as hedgehog cactus, a small, spiny cactus that produces bright, showy flowers in magentas, pinks, and scarlets.

Desert prickly pear cactus *(Opuntia, various species)*

A very widespread genus with about a dozen species that grow all over the arid West, prickly pear cactus is related to the cholla. In addition to being one of the most common plants of the Chihuahuan desert, prickly pear cactus can be found growing on hot cliff slopes as far north as the Upper Missouri River in Montana, very close to the Canadian border! Among the species of the Chihuahuan desert are bearded, blind, brown-spined, Engelmann, low, New Mexico, plains, purple, Santa Rita and tuberous.

The prickly pear has fleshy flat pads that help store water, enable photosynthesis, and produce flowers. Large spines grow from wartlike projections called tubercles. Unlike other cactuses, the *Opuntia* genus has another set of tiny spines called glochids, which grow just above the regular spines. They are hard to see, and equally hard to remove.

Flowers can be red, yellow, or violet; the mature plant varies in height from less than a foot to over seven feet tall, depending on species. The fruit, produced in spring and summer, makes delicious syrups and along with the pads (called nopales) is used in much Indian and southwest cuisine.

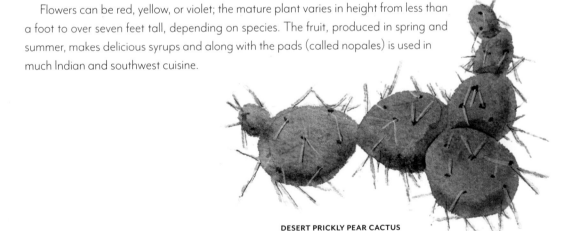

DESERT PRICKLY PEAR CACTUS

Fishhook barrel cactus *(Ferocactus wislizeni)*

The fishhook barrel cactus (opposite) is also called the Arizona barrel cactus, candy barrel cactus, and Southwestern barrel cactus. It has been known as the compass barrel because some of the larger specimens lean toward the southwest. It is native to northern Mexico and the Chihuahuan Desert in the United States. The reddish-yellow flowers and yellow fruit develop at the top of the plant. The seeds within the fruit are favored by desert birds, but bighorn sheep often break open the tough skin and eat the flesh of the cactus. The fishhook cactus is usually found along desert washes, not on slopes or valley floors, and grows to about six to ten feet tall in optimal conditions, but more often averaging two to four feet, with a diameter of eighteen to thirty inches.

California fan palm *(Washingtonia filifera)*

In the Coachella Valley a northwestern extension of the Sonoran Desert, east of Palm Springs and Palm Desert, lies the beautiful oasis of Thousand Palms Preserve.

From my journal of the trip:

When my friend and I drove to Thousand Palms Preserve northeast of Palm Desert, where we were staying with friends, we were startled by the size of the oasis—it was truly a thousand palms. Paul thought this expanse of verdant greens floating above the parched desert ochre and buff hues was like arriving in a different land. Being from the Pacific Northwest, and used to dark-hued conifers everywhere, I was utterly delighted by the novelty and peculiar character of this world— I had never before been to the desert nor had ever seen a palm oasis. Once on the trail, walking wide-eyed in the frond-striped shade beneath the towering sixty foot tall palms, I imagined dinosaurs around the corner and pterodactyls flying in formation overhead. It was so unreal that I felt like I was on a Hollywood set: was it Jurassic Park or King Kong?

The prehistoric connection wasn't only in our imaginations—it is real. California's plant distribution is extremely complex, and one small group of flora, the Neotropical Tertiary Geoflora, once covered the southern portion of North America. The Tertiary Period began around 40 million years ago and ended 10 million years ago. Plant life was composed of diverse tropical and subtropical trees like figs, avocados, cinnamon, palms and others. In more recent geologic time, much cooler and drier conditions existed in North America. Now the neotropical flora is mostly restricted to southern Mexico and northern South America; only relicts remain in southern North America—in places like desert palm oases.

The Thousand Palms Oasis Preserve is astride the San Andreas Fault, as well as sitting atop a huge underground aquifer that provides water to the Coachella Valley and cities beyond. This groundwater is the source of nourishment for the oasis; in some seasons it is supplemented by the rainwater and snowmelt from the Little San Bernardino Mountains to the east.

The California fan palm (page 179), also known as the desert palm, is the only palm tree native to western North America and is a member of the *Arecaceae* genus, and not actually a tree; this species is one that assumes a tree-like form. It has a large gray trunk without branches fissured with horizontal and some vertical lines, two to three feet in diameter. The tree grows from twenty to sixty feet high; along the top of the tree, fan-shaped evergreen leaves spread out, arranged on long stems. The fronds are three to five feet long, each with hooked spines along the edges. In the wild the old leaves cling to the tree forming long full skirts that reach the ground, making homes for bats, birds and other wildlife—these encumbered palm trunks are so much more beautiful than the more stereotypical palms you imagine in vacation settings, with dead leaves trimmed off, leaving long, elegant trunks. You can encounter an occasional bare trunk In the oasis because storms with high winds can blow leaves off in more exposed locations.

The Cahuilla Indians of southern California used the small black fruits of the palm as a flour. They also soaked the fruits to create sweet drinks and jellies. The palm fronds made roof thatching, and leaves were also used for weaving and for making sandals. The Thousand Palms oasis was an important gathering place for the Cahuilla, with its water source and plentiful trees.

> *In Xanadu, did Kubla Khan*
>
> *A stately pleasure-dome decree . . .*
>
> *And here were forests ancient as the hills,*
>
> *Enfolding sunny spots of greenery.*
>
> **—Samuel Taylor Coleridge,** from *Kubla Khan*

ENGELMANN SPRUCE AND SUBALPINE FIRS AT WASHINGTON PASS

Acknowledgments

I offer thanks to my family and friends, who've accompanied me on so many of my outdoor excursions: Tom, Rose, David, Paul, Jane, Julie, Gerry, Dave, Kendall, Ilona, and Martin.

For readers who offered me early ideas and encouragement: Paul Kasprzyk, Ilona Popper, Patrick Friel, and David Lord.

To Paul, for reading and sharing his editorial expertise and for his constant help throughout the writing and illustrating of this book.

To everyone who has assisted me in publishing:

Anne Depue, my agent, who supported and encouraged me all the way on four books.

Kate Rogers, editor in chief of Mountaineers Books, whose deep consideration helped shape my ideas and the form of the book.

Mary Metz, project editor, who kept me going in so many ways with good humor and great ideas.

Linda Gunnarson, development editor, who with great care and thoughtfulness helped me craft a book that fulfilled all my intentions.

Laura Lancaster, copy editor, who gave excellent suggestions for refining my prose.

Kate Basart, book designer who makes art look so beautiful.

Katie and Tom Burke and the rest of the staff at Pomegranate Publications; Cary Cartmill of Digital Canvas Northwest; photographer Gerry Fuller; poets John Daniel and Kim Stafford of Oregon, Ilona Popper of Montana, Tim McNulty and Saul Weisberg of Washington, and Jane Graham George of New Zealand; Ranger Christy Pendley, formerly of Crater Lake and Redwoods national parks; colleagues at the outdoor institutes where I teach: Christian Martin, Evan Holmstrom, and Saul Weisberg, director emeritus and founder of the North Cascades Institute, and Katie Roloson of the Yellowstone Forever Institute; librarians Brian Thompson, Rebecca Alexander, Jessica Anderson, and Laura Blumhagen at the Elisabeth C. Miller Library, University of Washington Botanic Gardens; and to my many students: you continue to inspire me. Special thanks to Stephen Whitney's *Western Forests* (in the National Audubon Society Nature Guide series), which I have consulted and used until it is dog-eared!

Glossary

Angiosperm: A plant that has flowers and produces seeds enclosed within a carpel. The angiosperms are a large group and include herbaceous plants, shrubs, grasses, and most trees.

Biogeographic realm: Also called an ecozone, this is a large area with particular flora and fauna that evolved as a result of their isolation during continental drift.

Biogeographic region: Also called an ecoregion, this is a geographic area with a unique combination of plants, animals, geology, climate, and water features.

Biomass: The total weight of all living organisms in a particular area.

Biome: A large, naturally occurring community of flora and fauna that occupy a major habitat. Worldwide, the major biomes include aquatic, tropical rainforest, deciduous and coniferous forest, grassland, desert, and tundra.

Boreal: Pertaining to the cool, moist coniferous forest region of northern North America as well as worldwide. In North America it stretches from Alaska to Newfoundland, and is also found in the alpine regions of the United States.

Broadleaf: Having wide leaves, generally in reference to deciduous trees.

Canopy: The uppermost level of a forest community.

Catkin: A compact and often drooping cluster of reduced, stalkless, and usually unisexual flowers.

Chaparral: Low, thick, scrubby growth consisting of evergreen shrubs or low trees, common in semiarid climates.

Climax: The plants and animals that persist in a given community as long as conditions remain stable.

Colonnade: A row of trees, often with stiltlike roots, that remain after the nurse log on which they grew as saplings has disappeared.

Conifer: A cone-bearing tree of the pine family.

Deciduous: Shedding leaves seasonally, and leafless for part of the year.

Duff: Decaying organic matter on the forest floor.

Ecosystem: A system of ecologically linked and mutually dependent animals and plants that have evolved together in a specific environment.

Ecotone: The transition area between two communities, containing species from each community as well as organisms unique to the transition area.

Gymnosperm: A plant that has seeds unprotected by an ovary or fruit. Gymnosperms include the conifers, cycads, and ginkgo.

Habitat: The place or community where a plant or animal naturally grows and lives.

Hardwood: Referring to broadleaved trees (angiosperms), as opposed to conifers (gymnosperms).

Herb: A plant with soft, not woody, stems that dies to the ground in the winter.

Krummholz: Stunted, windblown trees growing near the tree line on mountains. This German compound word is formed from *krumm*, which translates as crooked, bent, or warped, and *Holz*, which means wood.

Litter: The surface layer of the forest floor, consisting of slightly decomposed organic matter.

Nurse log: A fallen log or snag on which sprouts or seedlings begin to grow into new trees.

Samara: A dry, one-seed fruit with a wing, especially on maples.

Scrub: Stunted vegetation growing in sand or infertile soil.

Subspecies: A more or less distinct geographic population of a species that is able to interbreed with other members of the species.

Succession: An orderly sequence of plant and animal communities, with one group replacing another, ending in a climax or final stage.

Timberline: Also called the tree line, refers to a limit, created by climate topography or environment, above which trees cannot grow.

Tracheid: A type of water-conducting cell in the xylem that lacks perforations in its cell wall.

Understory: The lower layer of foliage in a forest, shaded by the canopy. Can also include middle- and lower-level plants, such as shrubs, flowers, and seedlings.

Venation: The arrangement of veins in a leaf or in an insect's wings.

Further Reading

FIELD GUIDES

Arno, Stephen F. *Northwest Trees: Identifying and Understanding the Region's Native Trees.* Illustrated by Ramona P. Hammerly. Seattle: Mountaineers Books, 1977.

DeMarco, Lois, and Jay Mengel. *Identifying Trees of the West: An All-Season Guide to Western North America.* Mechanicsburg, PA: Stackpole Books, 2015.

Franklin, Jerry F. *The Forest Communities of Mount Rainier National Park.* Washington, DC: Government Printing Office, 1988.

Franklin, Jerry F., and C. T. Dyrness. *Natural Vegetation of Oregon and Washington.* Washington, DC: Government Printing Office, 1973.

Jacobson, Arthur Lee. *Trees of Seattle.* Seattle: Jacobson, 2006.

Jensen, Edward C., and Charles R. Ross. *Trees to Know in Oregon.* Corvallis, OR: Oregon State University Press, 2005.

Kauffmann, Michael Edward. *Conifers of the Pacific Slope: A Field Guide to the Conifers of California, Oregon, and Washington.* Kneeland, CA: Backcountry Press, 2013.

Kauffmann, Michael Edward. *Conifer Country: A Natural History and Hiking Guide to the 35 Conifers of the Klamath Mountain Region.* Kneeland, CA: Backcountry Press, 2012.

Kircher, John. *A Field Guide to California and Pacific Northwest Forests.* Illustrated by Gordon Morrison. Boston: Houghton Mifflin, 1998.

Lanner, Ronald M. *Conifers of California.* Los Olivos, CA: Cachuma Press, 1999.

Lyons, C. P. *Trees and Shrubs of Washington.* Edmonton, AB: Lone Pine Publishing, 1999.

Ornduff Robert, and Phyllis M. Faber and Todd Keeler-Wolf. *Introduction to California Plant Life.* Berkeley: University of California Press, 2003.

Pielou, E. C. *The World of Northern Evergreens.* Ithaca, NY: Cornell University Press, 2011.

Pojar, Jim, and Andy MacKinnon. *Plants of the Pacific Northwest Coast: Washington, Oregon, British Columbia and Alaska.* Redmond, WA: Lone Pine Publishing, 1994

Quinn, Ronald, and Sterling C. Keeley. *Introduction to California Chaparral.* Berkeley: University of California Press, 2006.

Turner, Mark, and Ellen Kuhlmann. *Trees and Shrubs of the Pacific Northwest.* Portland, OR: Timber Press, 2014.

Whitney, Stephen. *National Audubon Society Nature Guides: Western Forests.* New York: Alfred A. Knopf, 1982.

Zobrist, Kevin W. *Native Trees of Western Washington: A Photographic Guide.* Pullman, WA: Washington State University Press, 2014.

NATURAL HISTORY

Arno, Stephen F. *Timberline: Mountain and Arctic Forest Frontiers.* Illustrated by Ramona P. Hammerly. Seattle: Mountaineers Books, 1984

Farjon, Aljos. *A Natural History of Conifers.* Portland, OR: Timber Press, 2008.

Luther, Kem. *Boundary Layer: Exploring the Genius Between Worlds.* Corvallis, OR: Oregon State University Press, 2017.

Mabey, Richard. *The Cabaret of Plants.* New York: W. W. Norton, 2017.

Peattie, Donald Culross. *Natural History of Western Trees.* Boston: Houghton Mifflin, 1953.

SPECIES ACCOUNTS

Arno, Stephen F., and Carl E. Fiedler. *Douglas Fir: The Story of the West's Most Remarkable Tree.* Seattle: Mountaineers Books, 2020.

Fiedler, Carl E., and Stephen F. Arno. *Ponderosa: People, Fire, and the West's Most Iconic Tree.* Missoula: Mountain Press, 2015.

Hartesveldt, R. J., H. T. Harvey, H. S. Shellhammer, and R. E. Stecker. *Giant Sequoias.* Three Rivers, CA: Sequoia Natural History Association. 1981.

Lanner, Ronald M. *Conifers of California.* Los Olivos, CA: Cachuma Press, 1999.

Pavlik, Bruce M., Pamela C. Muick, Sharon G. Johnson, and Marjorie Popper. *Oaks of California.* Los Olivos, CA: Cachuma Press, 2006.

Petersen, David. *Among the Aspen: Life in an Aspen Grove.* Flagstaff, AZ: Northland, 1991.

Peterson, Russell. *The Pine Tree Book*. Illustrated
  by Patricia Wynne. New York: Central Park
  Conservancy, 2004.
Rogers-Iversen, Kristen. *Interwoven: Junipers and the
  Web of Being*. Salt Lake City: University of Utah
  Press, 2018.

OTHER BOOKS

Carder, Al. *Giant Trees of Western America and the
  World*. Madeira Park, BC: Harbour Publishing,
  2005.
Florin, Lambert. *Historic Glimpses of Trees of the West*.
  Seattle: Superior Publishing, 1977.
Kimmerer, Robin Wall. *Gathering Moss: A Natural and
  Cultural History of Mosses*. Corvallis, OR: Oregon
  State University Press, 2003.

Mitchell, Alan. *The Trees of North America*. Illustrated
  by David More. New York: Facts on File, 1987.
Nadkarni, Nalini M. *Between Earth and Sky: Our
  Intimate Connections to Trees*. Berkeley: University of
  California
  Press, 2008.
Simard, Suzanne. *Finding the Mother Tree: Discovering
  the Wisdom of the Forest*. New York: Alfred A. Knopf,
  2021.
Stafford, Kim. *Singer Come from Afar: Poems*.
  Pasadena: Red Hen Press, 2021.
Van Pelt, Robert. *Forest Giants of the Pacific Coast*.
  Seattle: University of Washington Press, 2001.
Vaucher, Hugues. *Tree Bark: A Color Guide*. Portland,
  OR: Timber Press, 2003.

Supplies

The following list includes the materials that have performed best for me over the years.

ART MATERIALS STORES

There are countless online resources and some fine, well-stocked retail outlets for art supplies. I recommend that you shop at retail art stores to get the best advice. The sales staffs are almost always artists and love helping you find just what you need.
- Artist and Craftsman Supply, www.artistcraftsman.com
- John Neal Bookseller, www.johnnealbooks.com
- McClain's Printmaking Supplies (online only), www.imclains.com
- Paper and Ink Arts, www.paperinksarts.com
- University Bookstore, www.bookstore.washington.edu

DRAWING MATERIALS
- HB and 6B pencils; for field sketches and general sketching, mechanical pencils are ideal
- Staedtler white Mars Plastic eraser
- Pilot G-Tec pen, .38 and .5 nib width
- Stylist felt-tip pen; dissolves into a nice blue-black, excellent for quick sketches
- Staedtler brush pens, a variety of grays and browns
- Signo Uni-ball broad white pen, for small details on feathers and other highlights
- Posca white pen for small details
- Stillman & Birn archival-quality sketchbooks; available in spiral-bound and softbound, in white, ivory, gray, and tan. The colored papers are ideal for making sketches on toned paper with white gouache.

WATERCOLOR MATERIALS

- Watercolor papers: Arches 140 lb. cold press; Fabriano Artistico 140 lb. cold press; Lanaquarelle 140 lb. cold press; Saunders Waterford 140 lb coldpress. You can have these papers cut and spiral-bound into a sketchbook at an office supply store or specialty binder.
- Bristol or other drawing paper: 90 lb. weight (minimum) so it can handle a light watercolor wash
- Brushes: Da Vinci Maestro sable rounds, numbers 4 and 6, plus a ¾" wide flat sable brush and a ½" synthetic flat brush
- Palettes: John Pike Palette; San Francisco Slant Palette with multiple large wells for mixing washes
- Portable watercolor sets: Sennelier, Winsor & Newton, Van Gogh; alternatively, fill an Alvin travel palette with the paints listed below

Watercolor Tube Paints in Primary Colors
(a warm and a cool of each)

I prefer Daniel Smith watercolors. Other high-quality manufacturers are Winsor & Newton, Old Holland, Schmincke, Sennelier, and M. Graham.

- Blue: phthalo blue red shade, phthalo blue green shade
- Yellow: hansa yellow deep, hansa yellow medium
- Red: permanent alizarin crimson, pyrrol scarlet
- Other colors: cobalt blue, hansa yellow light, quinacridone burnt orange, carbazole violet, yellow ochre, perylene green, permanent white gouache

PRINTMAKING MATERIALS

- Safety-Kut carving blocks; available in various sizes but cheapest if you buy the biggest and cut your own
- Speedball carving tools and handle: tools numbers 1–5: U-gouge, big and small; V-gouge, big and small; square gouge
- Charbonnel etching inks: soft black, carbon black, and many other colors available
- Papers: Arches 140 lb. hot press; Fabriano Artistico 140 lb. hot press; Lanaquarelle 140 lb. hot press; Rives BFK printmaking for etching

PRINTMAKING COOPERATIVES AND STUDIOS (FOR CLASSES, WORKSHOPS, AND PRESS TIME)

Seattle, Washington:
- Pratt Fine Arts Center, www.pratt.org
- Print Zero Studios, www.printzerostudios.com

Bellingham, Washington:
- Runaway Press, www.runaway.press

Portland, Oregon:
- Flight 64 Studio, www.flight64.org
- Multnomah Arts Center, www.multnomahartscenter.org
- Print Arts Northwest, www.printartsnw.org

San Francisco, California:
- Graphic Arts Workshop, www.graphicartsworkshop.org
- 3Fish Studios, www.3fishstudios.com

Index

Page numbers in italic refer to illustrations

WESTERN HEMLOCK

About the Author

MOLLY HASHIMOTO explores parks and wildlife refuges all over the West, finding inspiration for her artwork in the natural world all around us. Her work has appeared for more than thirty years on cards and calendars published by Pomegranate Communications, and her previous books under the Skipstone imprint include *Colors of the West*, *Birds of the West*, and *Mount Rainier National Park: An Artist's Tour*.

Dedicated to connecting people with nature through hands-on art experiences, Molly Hashimoto teaches aspiring artists and has led plein air art workshops throughout the West, including at the North Cascades Institute, Yellowstone Forever Institute, Yosemite Conservancy, and Sitka Center for Art and Ecology. She lives in Seattle.

SKIPSTONE is an imprint of independent, nonprofit publisher Mountaineers Books. It features thematically related titles that promote a deeper connection to our natural world through sustainable practice and backyard activism. Our readers live smart, play well, and typically engage with the community around them. Skipstone guides explore healthy lifestyles and how an outdoor life relates to the well-being of our planet, as well as of our own neighborhoods. Sustainable foods and gardens; healthful living; realistic and doable conservation at home; modern aspirations for community—Skipstone tries to address such topics in ways that emphasize active living, local and grassroots practices, and a small footprint.

Our hope is that Skipstone books will inspire you to effect change without losing your sense of humor, to celebrate the freedom and generosity of a life outdoors, and to move forward with gentle leaps or breathtaking bounds.

All of our publications, as part of our 501(c)(3) nonprofit program, are made possible through the generosity of donors and through sales of 700 titles on outdoor recreation, sustainable lifestyle, and conservation. To donate, purchase books, or learn more, visit us online:

www.skipstonebooks.org
www.mountaineersbooks.org

SKIPSTONE
LIVE LIFE
MAKE RIPPLES

Also Available